TEA
FOR THE
PEOPLE

A guide to Britain's favourite brew
for home cooks, crafters and tea lovers.

MARC RILEY & OWEN TERRY

TEA
FOR THE
PEOPLE

©2022 Batch Tea Co. & Meze Publishing Ltd.
All rights reserved

First edition printed in 2022 in the UK

ISBN: 978-1-910863-79-4

Written by: Marc Riley, Owen Terry

Photography by: Tim Green

Edited by: Katie Fisher, Phil Turner

Designed by: Paul Cocker

Sales & PR: Emma Toogood, Lizzy Capps

Contributors: Lis Ellis, Megan Georgia,
Lizzie Morton

me:ze PUBLISHING

Published by Meze Publishing Limited
Unit 1b, 2 Kelham Square
Kelham Riverside
Sheffield S3 8SD
Web: www.mezepublishing.co.uk
Telephone: 0114 275 7709
Email: info@mezepublishing.co.uk

Printed in Great Britain
by Bell and Bain Ltd, Glasgow

GREETINGS TEA LOVER!

Firstly, a big THANKS for bagging yourself this book, or, if you received it as a gift, then a big thanks to the gifter for gifting it, and to you for opening it! We hope you enjoy reading it and getting stuck in to the recipes and activities as much as we enjoyed bringing them together for you (that's a lot, by the way).

We are Marc and Owen, of Batch Tea Co. We're two chaps who own a little tea company and think that tea is much more than we give it credit for. Tea is not only delicious and fun to drink, eat and experiment with, but inspiring in so many ways, from the beauty and the journey of the leaves themselves, to the history, the culture and the passion that has been the hallmark of enjoying tea for thousands of years, in various forms.

Thinking of the impact the humble leaf has had on individuals, cultures, politics – every area of life in some way – it's humbling to be a small part of the industry and try to have an impact in our own way.

We're passionate about educating the British public about the beauty and variety of tea out there since, although we think of ourselves as a tea-drinking nation, and British history is so intertwined with tea production, in the UK we're certainly not very knowledgeable about tea!

So, this book. What's it all about then?

Well, as tea lovers, we don't just drink our beloved leaf. Oh no! We love to experiment with tea. We bake with it, cook with it, infuse it into spirits and make kickass cocktails with it. We even make soap with it.

This book brings all these ideas together to create an inspirational collection of recipes we hope you'll love (or at least be intrigued by) so please DO try them at home.

And fear not, dear reader. The whole point of our business is to make tea more accessible to everyone, so you won't need any expensive equipment or skills outside of the ordinary to really get stuck in. If a bunch of new and exciting things to do with tea sounds interesting, this book is for you.

WE GET BY WITH A LITTLE HELP FROM OUR FRIENDS...

A huge part of developing this book and our business over the last couple of years has been our collaborations and the community – within and beyond the tea industry – forged by those connections.

We love working with people who share our ethos, inspire us and help us discover even more fun ways to use tea. Within these pages, you'll find some truly great independent businesses from across the UK and further afield. The wonderful creatives behind these indies have generously shared their expertise on everything from ice cream to gin, and soap to wall art for your perusal and enjoyment.

So, without further ado, please dig in and, most importantly, enjoy.

Marc & Owen x

CONTENTS

IN THE CUP

BLENDS

HOT DRINKS

COLD DRINKS

SPIRITS & COCKTAILS

TEA

AS WE THINK WE KNOW IT.

In the UK (as a sweeping generalisation…), we tend to think of tea as your standard bag of black tea, chucked in a mug with boiling water, a splash of milk and perhaps a sugar or two. There's nothing wrong with that, of course – we believe that the best way to drink tea is how YOU like it; not how someone tells you it should be drunk (and that goes for everything in life. Make your own kind of music. Sing your own special song. You get the gist) – but there's so much more to tea than your usual dusty teabag.

Overseas, a huge variety of teas are enjoyed in many different ways, with their own different stories, cultural heritage, traditions, quirks and even equipment. We want to bring some of that fascinating history, culture, science and versatility to more people at home.

A few tea facts to get you started:

All tea comes from the same plant, camellia sinensis, and much like any natural product it tastes better (and is better for you and the environment) when produced properly. Each of the recipes and activities in this book contains tea – camellia sinensis – in some form.

Like the grapes used to make wine, tea leaves are affected by the plant's genes and the varietal; the growing environment, including the soil, amount of sun, rain, wind or shelter it has had during its life; and the methods used to pick and process the leaf.

From the one plant, tea processing produces six main types of tea: white, green, yellow, oolong, black and aged or fermented tea.

When you add flavoured teas, like jasmine green, and blended teas, like English Breakfast, to the mix, some estimates put us at well over 20,000 different types of tea, but in theory this number is limitless due to small differences in processing and the constantly changing nature of the environment.

THE ART OF TEA

OR IS IT A SCIENCE?

The artistry of these processes is something we probably don't think about very much, but the amount of knowledge that traditional 'tea masters' hold, and the amount of culture, science, passion and understanding that goes in to making every single batch of tea is incredible when you start to understand what really goes on in those homesteads, processing plants or factories.

As weather conditions will differ every year, it's down to the tea master to produce a consistent flavour profile from the raw materials, and this takes years of dedication, passion and an intense understanding and "oneness" with the leaf to get right. To us, that's mind-blowing stuff.

While modern day soil analysis and the creation of the ideal conditions for tea agriculture is becoming an increasingly scientific procedure, every step in the different stages of tea processing performed by the artisan tea master – be it knowing the perfect time to prune and pick the leaves, when to stop the withering process and move to the "kill-green" stage, when to stop turning the leaves over by hand in the red-hot pan to get just the right amount of oxidation, the rolling of the leaves… everything – is done by sight, smell, and taste.

Each of these factors plays an important role in determining the final aroma, flavour profile, astringency and mouthfeel of the finished product. One process out of line can alter the quality of the finished tea no end.

TEA IS GOOD FOR ME

NOT ONLY IS TEA A BEAUTIFUL MARRIAGE OF ART AND SCIENCE, IT'S ALSO VERY GOOD FOR YOUR BODY, MIND AND SOUL!

We've all heard how white and green tea are full of antioxidants, which are brilliant for the immune system, and that we should drink more of these in our day to day lives, but we may not know much more than that.

In actual fact, all tea is packed full of antioxidants, not just green and white tea.

Additionally, Hei Cha – fermented teas such as Pu'er, Liu Bao or Fu Cha – offer myriad health benefits related to the microbial nature of the fermentation process. These teas are said to be excellent for heart health and cholesterol reduction, to aid digestion, regulate blood sugar levels and many more benefits.

Of course, the elephant in the room here is caffeine. Caffeine is a compound naturally found in tea leaves, in higher concentrations than in coffee (although your usual brew will likely contain less caffeine than its coffee counterpart, as you'll use around four times the weight of coffee than you would tea in one serving), and so all tea will contain caffeine unless it undergoes a decaffeinating process.

Caffeine's effect on the body is a short-term increase in alertness and reduced fatigue, which isn't necessarily a bad thing, in moderation of course. Caffeine's bad rep comes from over-indulgence and the famous "coffee shakes" or jitters from over consumption, or over-stimulation in an already stimulating world, leading to anxiety and stress.

However, the jitters are a rare phenomenon among tea drinkers due to tea's lower absolute caffeine content per brew, but also due to the presence of certain antioxidants and the amino acid L-Theanine, which has a profound relaxing effect.

Hence, your lovely brew can help to bring about a state of calm, while the gentle caffeine nudge can assist with improved focus and attention, resulting in the perfect combination of relaxation and mental alacrity that we need to go about our day.

Note: While your "regular" brew might not contain so much caffeine, watch out for matcha and other powdered teas, or recipes where you're eating or drinking the whole leaf! As you're consuming the entire leaf you're taking on everything it contains, including all the caffeine.

GOOD FOR THE SOUL, YOU SAY?

WELL, SINCE YOU ASKED...

There are a few ways that we'd consider our humble friend tea, to be particularly good for the soul.

Firstly, the simple process of making tea at home can create a mindful pause in our daily lives, allowing us a break from whatever we're toiling at, while creating a space for reflection, nature watching or just plain old doing nothing. Just sit back and enjoy the cuppa! These breaks are important to us, in an increasingly technologically connected world, and the chance to switch off and focus on preparing and enjoying a healthy drink can be vital in staving off that stress threshold.

Secondly, and related to this, we hark back to that L-Theanine/caffeine combo. L-Theanine is a compound found naturally in tea that has a profound effect on alpha brainwave activity. The mindfulness gurus among you may understand what this means, but to anybody else, alpha brainwaves are the type that usually occur when you're involved in such activities as daydreaming, meditating, or practicing mindfulness and a mounting body of research suggests that this type of brain wave can play an important role in reducing the symptoms of depression and increasing creativity.

Where else can you get your L-Theanine hit? Well, there are only three sources of theanines in nature, so, if you don't like tea, you might be better turning to meditation for your alpha brainwave promotion!

Thirdly, and arguably most importantly, the act of drinking tea is a time-honoured way of bringing people together, whether that's over a teapot with friends in the UK or a traditional ceremony elsewhere in the world.

As human beings, we're social animals, so there's not much more important for our welfare than community and social contact. So, the next time you're feeling a little down, pick up the blower, have someone pop round and pop the kettle on.

You'll be doing yourself the world of good.

STRIVING FOR A BETTER, MORE SUSTAINABLE BREW

Part of the reason we're so passionate about encouraging education around tea is twofold: we believe that there is so much quality tea out there that the public would LOVE, and also that there exists an opportunity to build a fairer, more harmonious world through the enjoyment of higher quality, sustainably produced teas.

We have to recognise that tea's history is not all sunshine, lollipops and rainbows. Intensive farming methods and poor employee rights in some tea producing nations, particularly former British colonies, have led to atrocious working conditions. Some countries still allow the use of pesticides and fertilisers banned in other areas for their effect on health. Unfortunately, these practices aren't all consigned to the history books just yet.

So, we want to educate people about the types of tea that are out there and how you can find a brew that's better for the farmer, the environment and you.

Unfortunately, there is no certification or industry standard that provides a universal panacea for the ills of decades of commodity farming practices. Organic, FairTrade and other certifications can only go so far, and many small farmer producers who use natural farming methods to produce the cleanest, highest quality teas available, could never afford these certifications. In buying from artisan tea companies who know their producers and the methods used, we can start to work against the tide, even if they can't show all the certifications.

And if you're buying commodity teas from the supermarket – because, let's face it, we're human and only have so much time and money – then please do look out for Ethical Tea Partnership, Fairtrade or Organic certifications. They might not be perfect but they're better than nothing.

TEA FOR THE PEOPLE

In line with the recent revolutions for craft beer, natural wine, single-origin coffee, et cetera, we know there's a growing interest in food and drink stories. Their origins, quality over quantity, what's in them and more are being investigated, giving us consumers a better understanding of the ethical and environmental implications of those products, as well as what's going into our bodies.

The power of these informed choices results in tea that is better for people, the planet, and the tea industry. A great example of this is the recent move towards biodegradable and plastic-free teabags, or ethical partnerships, in huge companies that have had to step up because people expect more and are seeking out smaller producers with better practices to compete against them.

In short, there's so much to learn about tea and its fascinating history, culture, versatility and properties. We could go on (and on) but really we just want people to think a little differently about this everyday staple, and hopefully get excited by all the possibilities it offers – not just in our cups, but on our plates and around our homes too.

Experiment, have fun, discover what you like and don't be afraid to try new things.
"Tea for the People" means tea for everyone, any time, any how, anywhere.

What you waiting for then? Stick the kettle on and have a nice brew while you flick through this book and decide what you're going to jump into first!

TEA TIPS

COOKING TIPS

Grind tea leaves in a spice or coffee grinder and add them to your other favourite herbs and spices to make a spice rub. Teas that work well with savoury foods include green tea, matcha, Darjeeling black teas and Earl Grey. Mix 2 tablespoons of ground tea with half a teaspoon of salt and a quarter teaspoon of black pepper plus whatever spices take your fancy.

Use tea in place of water: brew the tea and let it cool to room temperature,
then use it in any recipe that calls for water.

Use brewed tea to cook wholegrains like rice, quinoa or bulgur wheat.
Try cooking pasta in green tea!

Use brewed black or oolong tea to poach fruit such as peaches or pears.

Infuse your milk with tea to make a flavoursome morning porridge.

Make tea-infused olive oil. Add lemon, garlic or herbs to the oil along with your favourite teas, then simmer over a medium heat for 2 minutes. Turn off the heat, cover the saucepan with lid and allow the oil to infuse for 2 hours until cooled completely.

Add tea leaves directly to dishes while they are cooking or brew the leaves and then chop finely before stirring them in. Use them in the same way as dried herbs like oregano or thyme.

Mix chopped tea leaves into breadcrumbs or seasoned flour for coating meats and fish.

Add brewed tea to marinades and use it to marinate meats, fish, tofu, tempeh or vegetables.

Use powdered tea like matcha in any recipe using flour.
Just replace 1 teaspoon of flour in every 250g with matcha.

Use tea to add depth to vegetable stock for soups and casseroles. Adding teabags to a stew will create a delicious flavour base. Try something like Lapsang Souchong to bring out smoky notes.

GENERAL TIPS

Used tea leaves are full of nitrogen so they make a great fertiliser for the garden.
They're also great to use in wormeries.

Freshly used teabags work brilliantly as a hot or cold compress for tired eyes.
They can also help soothe minor eye injuries, dryness and inflammation.

Tea is very effective at absorbing odours.
Place used, dried teabags in your shoes and boots to get rid of nasty smells.

The tannin in black tea can help bring the natural colour back to dark woods when used as polish.
Try using a damp teabag to polish wood and then buff with a dry cloth to shine.

IN THE CUP

Tea "in the cup" is a very traditional way to enjoy camellia sinensis. It's certainly the most common – and almost the only – form of tea we find here in the UK. Offering family, friends and even the builder or plumber a cuppa when they step through your door, warming the teapot and keeping it piping hot with a tea cosy as it brews, milk jugs and little jars or cubes of sugar… however you serve tea, and wherever that sits on the scale of formality and etiquette, the act of presenting guests (or being presented) with this hot drink will probably be very familiar to you. We're also partial to afternoon tea, that very British meal of mini sandwiches and cakes somewhere between lunch and dinner, which often marks something to celebrate these days and might even feature glasses of fizz alongside the ubiquitous teapot.

What makes these experiences universal is how they bring people together, and this in turn is something you find in tea cultures everywhere. Hundreds of ceremonies and various brewing methods, whether formal events or everyday practices, exist around the world and yet, in essence, they all come down to sitting round a pot of tea together. For example, the Japanese tea ceremony of chado was sometimes used to get opposing generals into a hut without their armour, so they could discuss whether they needed to do battle, a practice that averted many wars according to the stories… Japanese matcha, Indian masala chai and Moroccan mint tea are just a few more examples where ceremony or performance plays a big part in the tea making process.

Whether you're whisking powdered tea in a bowl, steeping whole leaves in a pot or boiling tea with other ingredients in a saucepan, traditional brewing methods like these are well established and more widely known than ever before. In the UK there has also been a more recent emergence of other ways to make tea, from lattes to cocktails and the growing 'ready to drink' market which includes cold drinks like bubble tea, kombucha and bottled iced tea. The recipes in this section will take you through blends, hot and cold drinks, tea-infused spirits and cocktails to try at home – give them a go and you might just discover a new favourite!

BLENDS

Blended tea is the most consumed tea type in the world, especially here in the UK, where around 95% of tea consumption is a standard black tea blend such as English Breakfast.

So what is a tea blend? It's basically any tea that is made up of two or more varieties of tea. There are, therefore, infinite possibilities! What you create or what you like all depends on personal taste.

At an industrial level, blending is used to achieve the same flavour profile over time to suit customer needs, despite seasonal changes in the individual teas themselves due to weather conditions and other environmental factors.

The tea master has this difficult and highly skilled job, but at home all you need to do is throw a couple of teas into a container, shake them up and see what it tastes like! Blending your own tea really is that easy; even English Breakfast – probably the most famous blend in the world and synonymous with tea here in the UK – has no set recipe or even specific types of tea that must be included.

There are a few ways to approach blends. You could start by thinking of a tea you want to create, and then consider the flavours that could go into that, or go for something unique within a specific category – your own version of an Earl Grey, perhaps – which is probably going to be trickier but a good challenge! Within these approaches, you could either mix the dry leaves before brewing your blend and tasting, then amend the recipe and repeat the process to refine the flavour, or you could brew your chosen teas separately and then mix different amounts of the tea liquor to your liking.

However you choose to approach blending, remember that it's an experiment with no correct answer; only an exploration of what you do and don't like. These recipes are guides but not a rulebook, so focus on the flavours you want to achieve and remember to write down the versions you like so you can recreate them!

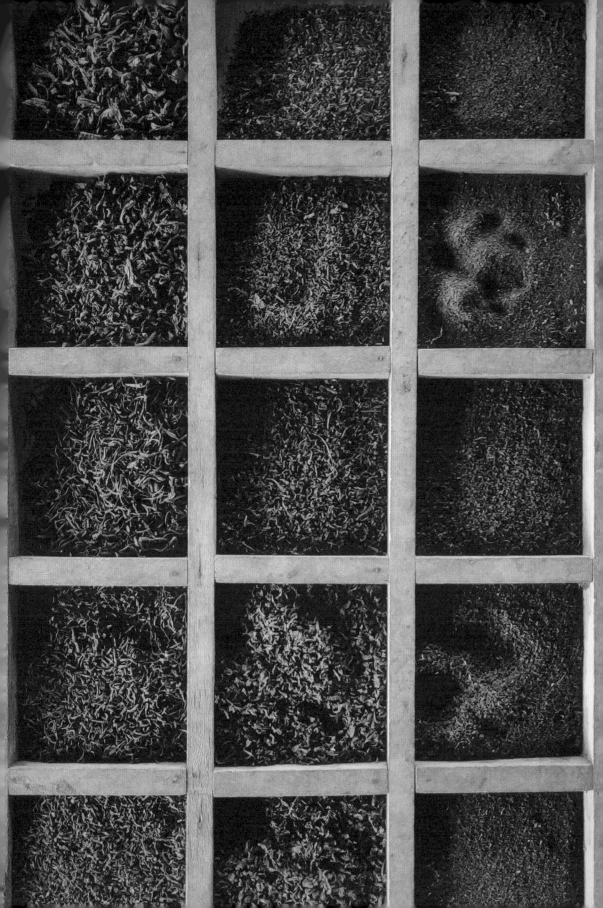

PUNCHY BREAKFAST BLEND

Preparation time: 5 minutes

Batch Tea Co's award-winning, signature breakfast blend was developed to have strength, depth and body while retaining the flavour notes of some of the more delicate whole leaf breakfast blends which are gracing tearooms and cafés these days. We blend a number of different Assam teas to create a fruity, malty base. However, for the purposes of this recipe you can just use your favourite, strong, biscuity flavoured leaf.

80% strong malty Assam
15% Darjeeling 2nd Flush
5% Ceylon Uva

A strong builder's brew first thing in the morning is hard to beat. Rich, malty and thick, all in the space of a couple of minutes thanks to our friend, the teabag. All that flavour is possible in such a short time because the tea which you find in most teabags is a type of tea called fannings. The leaf is crushed, torn and curled and cut up really small, meaning that there's a huge surface area for the water to steep. However, as tea shops have become more popular, loose leaf has made a resurgence, and more specifically there's been a growing movement towards whole leaf (i.e. not crushed and torn up) tea.

While we're all for whole leaf tea, what you gain in quality and flavour you often lose in 'quick' strength and convenience. Batch Breakfast was developed to bridge that gap and provide a strong black tea blend with high quality leaves packed full of flavour.

The method for blending a tea like this is simple. Take the required proportions and thoroughly mix in a container. That's about it! Be aware that if you are blending large whole leaves with finely broken leaves, then the smaller particles of tea may settle out of the blend and fall to the bottom of your container.

Experimenting with blends is what it's all about. Try the teas individually and then mix them to bring aspects of each flavour at different strengths into the blend. We use the Assam teas to bring body and malty depth, the Uva adds a floral and slightly astringent sweetness while the Darjeeling brings a lighter muscatel grape flavour to round out the other elements.

WITCH'S BREW

Preparation time: 10 minutes, plus drying overnight // Makes approx. 150g

The Steel Cauldron is Sheffield's very own wizarding and witchcraft fantasy café. Speaking to them about tea gave us a great opportunity to come up with something special that looked great and tasted even better. The concoction we created blends biscuity black tea with chocolate, vanilla and apricot notes, accompanied by sparks of colour from blue cornflower and fiery red safflower petals.

100g loose leaf biscuity black tea

A few sprays of good quality apricot extract

30g organic cocoa nibs

5-10g organic cocoa husks

5-10g vanilla seeds and pods, finely chopped (or a few sprays of vanilla extract)

2g cornflower petals

2g safflower petals

Add the tea to a container or bowl and use a kitchen mister to spray the extract(s) onto the tea. Mix the leaves as you are spraying and remember a little goes a long way! Add a sheet of kitchen towel to your container and leave overnight in a dry place to allow the water in the extract to evaporate.

The next day, add the cocoa nibs and husks, vanilla pods (if using) and petals to your dry flavoured tea leaves. Mix thoroughly. As with any blend, make yourself a cup to taste and adjust the quantities as you see fit, then serve and enjoy!

Tips

When using liquids like extract to add flavour to tea, you need to be very careful to use it sparingly and to allow the tea to dry properly. Adding liquid to dry tea leaves will soften the tea flavour and allowing moisture to remain in the tea will not only degrade the tea quicker, but it could also allow bacteria to flourish.

SENCHA BLOSSOM

Preparation time: 5 minutes // Makes 100g

Flavouring a tea with fruit, herbs or spices always brings out a delicate balance of flavours, but should be done to personal preference. In this recipe, the vegetal grassy notes of the sencha blend beautifully with the fruity, floral notes of the raspberry, rose and elderflower accompanied by flashes of colour from the vibrant blue cornflower. Getting hold of ingredients like elderflower is easy enough these days using online shopping or, if you have a dehydrator, go foraging and see what you can come up with. There's no wrong way really, so get out there and experiment!

88g loose leaf Japanese Sencha

5g dried raspberries

5g rose flowers

1g elderflower blossom

1g cornflower petals

Lightly chop the dried raspberries and add them to the sencha with the remaining flowers and petals. Give the mix a good stir and you're ready to go.

To brew the sencha blossom tea, spoon 3g of the mixture into each cup and cover with water at 80°c. Steep for around 2 minutes, or according to specific instructions for the sencha, before straining and drinking.

Sassy Noir

Breakfast Blend

Witch's Brew

Sencha Blossom

Sufganiyot

SUFGANIYOT TEA BOMBS

Preparation time: 1 hour // Cooking time: 10-15 minutes // Makes 10

◇◇◇

Sufganiyot are delicious Jewish doughnuts bursting with jam, dusted in icing sugar and served at Hanukkah. This recipe, created by our friend Peebs, encapsulates the joy of biting into a soft sufganiyot during these celebrations. An awesome and fun way to store your tea if you're bored of teabags!

◇◇◇

10g toasted coconut chips

5g freeze-dried strawberries

5g freeze-dried raspberries

10g Batch Tea's Java Black

18g vanilla rooibos tea

19g almond nibs

300g ready-tempered colourless isomalt (this is a sugar substitute that you can easily find in any good home baking store or online)

Equipment

You will also need 2 sheets of 10 small dome-shaped silicone moulds for this recipe.

In a food processor, pulse the coconut chips until roughly chopped (to about 2mm pieces) and then combine the coconut with all the remaining ingredients except the isomalt in a medium-sized bowl. Mix together thoroughly then set aside while you prepare the isomalt casing.

Place the isomalt into a heatproof bowl and heat in the microwave in 10 second bursts, stirring in between each burst, until the isomalt has melted. It should not be brought to the boil, as the isomalt may crystallise. Using a silicone pastry brush, brush the melted isomalt into the domes of the moulds. You will need to work fast as isomalt sets quickly, though you can always put it back in the microwave if required. Once done, leave the domes to set on a flat surface for 30 minutes.

Turn the isomalt domes out onto a clean surface. They should feel slightly tacky to the touch.

Spoon 1 teaspoon of the sufganiyot tea into half of the domes. Set a frying pan over a medium heat and lightly place an empty isomalt dome into the frying pan. Remove once you feel the edges melting slightly. Place the dome on top of one of the filled domes, making sure you line up the edges, to create an isomalt sphere. Repeat with the remaining domes until you have 10 tea bombs.

To serve

Place a sufganiyot tea bomb into a mug and pour boiling water (at 100°c) over the top, then watch the magic happen for 4-6 minutes while your tea brews. Make sure you stir the tea before you drink it to make sure all of the isomalt has dissolved into the water.

Tips

The tea blend by itself can be frozen and stored for up to 6 months, and the tea bombs can be stored in the fridge for up to 2 weeks. Use boiling water to clean your equipment, as this will melt the isomalt.

SWEET & FRAGRANT STICKY CHAI

Preparation time: 20 minutes // Makes approx. 100g sticky chai (enough for around 8 servings)

Adding honey to a great chai mix creates the most wonderful, unctuous chai drink in the world! The honey soaks up the spices and the tea soaks up the honey. Brew in the pan for a very special Sunday morning treat! Hygge in a cup.

For the chai mix

15g cinnamon bark

5g green cardamom pods

2 whole star anise

1g whole cloves or ½ tsp ground cloves

0.5g freshly ground nutmeg

1 tsp ground ginger

Pinch of salt

35g loose leaf CTC Assam black tea

40g clear honey

To serve (makes 1 mug):

200ml boiling water

200ml cold milk (dairy or plant-based)

A little sugar, to taste (optional)

For the chai mix

Weigh out your ingredients and heat a heavy-based pan over a medium heat. The secret to great chai is toasting your spices before blending. This brings out the oils and makes a much more fragrant and delicious drink. Be careful not to burn the spices though as this may make your mix a little acrid.

Bash the cinnamon into small pieces using a pestle and mortar, bash the cardamom gently to open the pods and break up the star anise. Toast all the whole spices individually in the hot pan, as they will all take different amounts of time. Cinnamon bark is pretty tough so takes longest (around 1-2 minutes) and star anise takes around 20 seconds. Cloves and cardamom pods only take around 10 seconds to release those beautiful fragrances and make your kitchen smell amazing!

Combine the toasted spices in a big bowl, add the ground spices along with the salt and tea, then mix everything together. Coat the mix in the honey and stir really well for a few minutes to ensure there are no dry clumps left.

Pop the sticky chai blend into a jar, seal with a lid and leave until ready to use. It will keep for a long time and may dry out after a few days but will still taste the same for over a year. It never lasts that long though because you'll drink it all much sooner!

To serve

You can make this in a pan, as a chai latte (see the tea lattes on page 34) or simply steeped with or without a splash of milk. We just love it in the pan. Here's how to do it.

Bring the water to the boil in a saucepan and then turn off the heat. Add 2 teaspoons of your sticky chai mix and leave to infuse for at least 3 minutes, longer if you have time.

Add the cold milk and heat gently, stirring constantly (or as often as seems sensible) until the milk starts to bubble and froth. Turn off the heat and leave to infuse for a couple of minutes. Strain the chai into your favourite mug, add a little sugar if you wish, find a quiet place and melt away.

Tips

Add a big teaspoon of cocoa husks to the pan for extra smooth, chocolatey heavenliness! You can also add half a teaspoon of freshly ground coffee to the pan for a brew with a kick.

HOT DRINKS

There's so much more to a cup of tea than just pouring hot water on a teabag...

There are so many possibilities out there for different flavourings to add, different methods of preparation and even different temperatures to brew your leaves at.

One important takeaway from this collection of recipes is to recognise the importance of water temperature and understand that different teas brew best at different temperatures.

So many people tell us they don't like green tea "because it's too bitter". What they're probably experiencing is a combination of poor-quality tea and preparing the tea at overly high temperatures; green tea needs to be brewed at a lower temperature (around 80°c) otherwise the hotter water brings out all those bitter notes that can taste, frankly, unpleasant. Traditionally, white tea is brewed at even lower temperatures (around 70°c) although that can be down to personal taste, and oolong sits somewhere between 80 and 95°c.

There are two other factors in brewing tea that can be adjusted to change the flavour: the amount of tea leaves you use, and the amount of time you leave it to steep for. The biggest piece of advice we can give is to experiment and find out what suits your personal tastes. The same goes for how to serve your tea: steamed milk, cold milk, sugar, sweetener… it's all up to you.

PROPER MOROCCAN MINT TEA

Preparation time: 10 minutes // Cooking time: 5 minutes // Serves 4

Moroccan mint tea, prepared properly, is a wonderful thing. The spectacle of the stunning teapots and glasses along with the skilful high pour is something to behold and the sweet, frothy, minty green tea is so refreshing after a meal. If you've ever had the real thing, you'll know that a so-called Moroccan Mint teabag is not even from the same species! Making it this way will transport you right to the lively cafés and bustling souks of North Africa.

2 tbsp loose leaf gunpowder green tea

1 litre water at 100°c

1 bunch of mint, stalks and all

1 ½ tbsp sugar

Generally, gunpowder green tea is used in Morocco for its distinctive strong, smoky flavour. It's inexpensive and can be found in most Asian supermarkets, but you can use other green teas. The traditional recipe uses a lot of tea to steep, and then balances the bitterness with a lot of sugar, so it should be served nice and sweet to be enjoyed after a meal. Of course, you can adjust the sugar content to your taste. Ideally you'll have a Moroccan tea set with tea glasses to serve this in, but it is possible to make in a regular teapot with small cups.

Add the tea leaves to your teapot and pour in enough hot water to just cover them. Leave for around 30 seconds then strain into a tea glass and keep the liquid. This is the 'spirit'. Add more hot water to cover the leaves again, swill the pot for 30 seconds or so, and then discard this liquid.

Now bung in the mint and sugar, pour your 'spirit' back into the pot and fill the teapot with the hot water. Stir well and place the teapot on a low-medium heat for about 3 minutes before pouring the tea into your glasses. When pouring, start close to the glass then raise the teapot as high as you can, still pouring and being careful not to cover the whole table, or any guests, in hot tea!

Once the glasses have been filled, pour the tea from all glasses back into the pot and pour again. Repeat this process 2 or 3 times. Pour one last time and enjoy your frothy, minty, sweet treat!

TEA LATTES

Lattes aren't just the reserve of "the other hot drink" you know. Tea makes a whole host of delicious lattes with myriad flavours from different teas and blends combining beautifully with creamy steamed milk to create a whole range of frothy mugs of heavenliness.

The basic premise of making a tea latte is this: Steep the tea leaves in a small amount of hot water (around 70-100ml) at the correct temperature for the tea type. Strain the tea and pour on hot steamed cow's milk or a plant-based alternative like oat or soya.

No fancy coffee machine with frother/steamer attachment? No worries! Did you know that you can create café-quality frothed milk using a cafetière (also known as a French Press) in just a few seconds? Simply heat your milk of choice in a pan or microwave, pour into your cafetière and slowly pump the plunger a few times until the milk has doubled in volume. Pour onto your steeped and strained tea for the perfect, velvety latte.

We've chosen four of our favourite Tea Latte recipes to share here.

STRAIGHT UP MALTY ASSAM LATTE

5g strong, malty loose leaf Assam (such as a CTC BOP grade)

100ml water at 100°c

200ml frothed milk of your choice

Steep your tea leaves in the hot water for around 3 minutes, then strain and top with the hot frothed milk. For a fragrant twist, add 3 or 4 lightly bashed green cardamom pods when steeping your tea leaves for an easy and delicious Cardamom Chai Latte.

STICKY CHAI LATTE

15g (2 heaped tsp) Kama Sutra Sticky Chai

100ml water at 100°c

200ml frothed milk of your choice

Sugar or honey to taste (optional)

Cinnamon or chocolate powder (optional)

Steep the sticky chai in the hot water for as long as possible (3 minutes minimum) before straining and topping with the hot frothed milk. Add a little sugar or honey for extra sweetness, then dust with cinnamon or chocolate powder for extra loveliness. If you like your lattes boozy, splash in a little Baileys, brandy or scotch to warm your cockles!

Straight Up Malty
Assam Latte

Sticky Chai
Latte

London Fog

Matcha Latte

MATCHA LATTE

3g (1 tsp) high quality organic matcha

3 tbsp water at 70°c

200ml frothed milk of your choice

Sugar, honey or vanilla syrup to taste (optional)

Put the matcha and hot water into your mug and whisk to a smooth paste. It's worth spending a couple of quid on a matcha whisk to smooth out the paste before adding milk, ensuring there are no big green lumps in your drink! Top with the frothed milk and add sweetener to taste.

Notes: Good quality matcha shouldn't really need sweetening but most of the matcha you'll find in the UK for under £30 per 100g may need a little sugar or vanilla syrup. For a beautiful summer drink, top the matcha paste with ice and cold milk instead of hot frothed milk, sweetening as per the hot version if needed.

LONDON FOG

4g (1 heaped tsp) loose leaf Earl Grey tea

100ml water at 100°c

20ml vanilla syrup

200ml frothed milk of your choice

To be honest, when we first heard about Earl Grey lattes we baulked slightly, wondering how the citrus would play against the creamy milk, but you know what? It's really tasty. The combination works beautifully and creates such a soothing drink to see you through the winter.

Simply steep your tea leaves in the hot water for around 3 minutes, strain and stir in the vanilla syrup, then top with the hot frothed milk.

If you're looking for the ultimate taste of Christmas, try adding a shot of Brandy de Jerez or Cognac for what we call Le Fog Parisienne. It's unbelievable. Make a big vat of this and serve it at your Christmas party to leave your guests with a very warm fuzzy feeling inside!

SADIA UR-REHMAN'S PAKISTANI ELAICHI CHAI

Preparation time: 5 minutes // Cooking time: 10 minutes // Makes 4 cups

Tea drinking has become an important part of everyday life in Pakistan; it's embedded in the culture and social life. This recipe is from artist Sadia Ur-Rehman and harks back to her visits to her parents' hometown in Pakistan where tea has played a pivotal role. It also epitomises the hospitality that guests receive; visitors would expect a cup of tea as a minimum.

750ml water

10-12 green cardamom pods

4 heaped tsp loose leaf black tea

4 tsp sugar

250ml milk

Bring your water to the boil in a saucepan. Split your cardamom pods and add them to the pan. Add the tea leaves and sugar, simmer for a minute then add the milk and boil until the tea is a creamy caramel colour.

Remove the pan from the heat and pour the chai into teacups, ensuring you use a strainer to catch the tea leaves and cardamom. Those can just be discarded.

This tea goes perfectly with almond and pistachio biscuits.

MATCHA GOLDEN MILK

Preparation/Cooking time: 5 minutes // Makes 2 mugs

Since the rise of turmeric as an all-round good guy and super-spice, golden milk has become a go-to drink for the health conscious. We love to add matcha for an extra antioxidant hit and that welcome pop of caffeine! Leave out the matcha for a soothing bedtime mug.

1 tsp organic matcha

600ml milk of your choice (coconut milk works brilliantly)

4cm turmeric root, sliced (or 1 ½ tsp ground turmeric)

1cm fresh ginger, sliced (or ½ tsp ground ginger)

1 cinnamon quill (or ½ tsp ground cinnamon)

1 tsp sugar (or honey, maple syrup or agave to taste)

If using, first put your matcha into a saucepan with a small amount of warm milk and whisk to create a smooth paste.

Pour the remaining milk, all the spices and your chosen sweetener into the pan, then heat until hot but not boiling. Turn off the heat and leave to infuse for a further minute or two before straining into mugs. Enjoy!

Tips

For an iced version, use ground spices. Whizz them with the matcha in a little warm water, then pour the mixture over ice and top with cold milk of your choice.

Elaichi Chai

Matcha Golden Milk

Golden Milk

HEALTHY TEA & HERB INFUSIONS

Preparing tea with other herbs has long been a staple of Ayurvedic discipline which itself is thousands of years old, promoting the health and wellbeing of body, mind and spirit. These simple recipes offer great tasting drinks that will heal your body and soul!

The method for all the infusions below is the same, as follows: Pour the freshly boiled water into a large bowl or pan, add the tea and remaining ingredients, then leave everything in the water as it cools. Either drink warm after the infusion has been steeping for about 5 minutes or allow it to cool completely and enjoy cold throughout the day.

BLACK TEA, BASIL & GINGER

1 litre water at 100°c

10g loose leaf Pai Mu Dan, greenish oolong or a light black tea

10 fresh basil leaves

15 fresh mint leaves

2cm root ginger, sliced into discs

3 cloves

CHAMOMILE, BASIL & ROSE GREEN TEA

1 litre water at 80°c

3g loose leaf green tea

2g chamomile flowers

2g tulsi (holy basil)

2g rose petals

5g dried orange peel

WHITE TEA, RASPBERRY & MINT

1 litre water at 80°c

10g loose leaf white tea

10 fresh raspberries

20 fresh mint leaves (stalks on is fine)

1 tsp cut liquorice root

GREEN TEA WITH TURMERIC & LEMON

1 litre water at 80°c

10g loose leaf green tea

2cm (around 5g) turmeric root, sliced into discs, or ¾ tsp dried turmeric

2cm (around 10g) root ginger, sliced into discs

½ lemon, juiced

Black Tea, Basil & Ginger

Green Tea with Turmeric & Lemon

White Tea, Raspberry & Mint

COLD DRINKS

As we explained in the previous chapter, tea is affected by the temperature it's brewed at, and this chapter demonstrates that cold – whether that's ambient or fridge – is just another temperature that gives different and equally wonderful results, combined with increased brewing time.

When preparing cold tea-based drinks, you can either brew the tea hot and then leave it to cool (just remember that flavours are more muted when drinks are cold, so the tea will need brewing stronger for best results) or use cold water and leave it to "cold infuse" for a longer time.

BLACKBERRY TEA COOLER

Preparation time: 15 minutes // Makes 2 glasses

◇◇

A super refreshing summer cooler made from green tea with blackberries, mint and lemon.

◇◇

5g loose leaf green tea

65g fresh blackberries, plus 2 extra for garnish

Handful of fresh mint leaves, plus 2 sprigs for garnish

800ml water at 80°c

1 tbsp sugar

Ice cubes

2 slices of lemon

Steep your green tea, blackberries and mint leaves (reserving the garnish) in the hot water for around 10 minutes. During this time, add the sugar and stir until dissolved.

Strain the liquid into a jug and leave in the fridge until really cold. Serve the cooler in tall glasses over ice and garnish each one with a slice of lemon, a fresh blackberry and a sprig of mint.

BUBBLE TEA TEARISTA SOFIE

Bubble Tea shops have popped up in all major cities recently with an array of sweet, flavoured milk teas and colourful boba options. But it really is easy, and much cheaper, to make bubble tea at home. Our good friend Sofie Vercauteren, aka Tearista Sofie, provided one of these delicious recipes for us straight from her exclusive Tearista service in Belgium. The other is one of our own favourites.

Feel free to experiment with a range of different teas, sweetness levels, boba pearl types and even milk types. You can use any tea you like: jasmine green, Hojicha, matcha, Taiwan oolong and black teas are particular favourites. The same goes for milk; Sofie uses soya milk in these recipes but feel free to try full-fat, semi-skimmed or even add a little cream or condensed milk! If you have a sweet tooth then you could also add some simple syrup, honey or agave to taste.

You can buy a variety of tapioca pearls from most oriental supermarkets, but be aware that they are not all the same. They require different cooking times, from 5 minutes right up to an hour, so we'd advise you to follow the packet instructions for the pearls that you buy.

MATCHA BUBBLE TEA LATTE

Preparation time: 10 minutes, plus cooling // Cooking time: 5 minutes, plus time to cook tapioca pearls // Serves 1

60g sweet tapioca pearls

130g ice cubes

100ml water at 80°c

3g matcha

100ml sweetened soya milk

You will need a milk foamer for this recipe.

Cook your tapioca pearls according to the packet instructions. Allow them to cool, then place in your glass and add your ice cubes.

Pour the hot water onto the matcha and whisk until lump-free. Pour this over your ice and pearls.

Foam your soya milk until rich and frothy then pour over the tea. Save the foam to layer on top of the drink. Sprinkle with matcha powder to finish, and enjoy!

ASSAM BLACK CARAMEL BOBA TEA WITH VANILLA FOAM

Preparation time: 5 minutes, plus cooling // Cooking time: 10 minutes, plus time to cook tapioca pearls // Serves 1

6g loose leaf Assam black tea

250ml water at 100°c

60g caramel tapioca pearls

130g ice cubes

100ml vanilla soya milk (if you can't find this then just add 10ml vanilla syrup to regular sweetened soya milk)

You will need a milk foamer for this recipe.

Steep your tea in the boiling water for 3 minutes, then strain. The leaves can be discarded. Leave the tea to cool.

Cook your tapioca pearls according to the packet instructions. Allow them to cool, then place in your glass and add your ice cubes. Pour 100ml of your cooled tea over the ice.

Foam your soya milk until rich and frothy, and pour into the tea. Save the foam to layer on top of the drink.

Matcha Bubble Tea Latte

Assam Black Caramel Boba Tea with Vanilla Foam

CLASSIC ICED TEA

Preparation time: 15 minutes, plus 1-2 hours cooling // Makes 1 litre

There's nothing more refreshing on a hot day than a classic iced tea in a tall glass packed full of ice with a slice of lemon and a sprig of mint. Sit in the garden, put your feet up and go to your happy place.

10g Lover's Leap Ceylon Tea

600ml boiling water

1 ½ tbsp sugar

500ml cold water or ice

1 ½ lemons, juiced

To serve

Ice

Lemon slice

Mint sprig

Straw (optional, but definitely completes the feel!)

Infuse the tea in the freshly boiled water for around 10 minutes. This will create a very strong brew. The cooling process dampens flavour, so you want it strong to make sure the taste comes through. You'll balance the bitterness with sugar and lemon.

Strain your strong tea infusion into a jug, pan or teapot. Add the sugar and stir to dissolve, then decant the mixture into your serving vessel. Add the cold water or ice and then let the tea cool to room temperature. Pop it in the fridge for an hour or so, if possible, to cool further.

Add the lemon juice to the chilled tea and stir well. Serve in a glass packed full of ice with the slice of lemon and sprig of mint to garnish.

Tips: If you're the organised type or live somewhere you can plan for hot weather, try cold infusing your Classic Iced Tea overnight for a smoother bevvie instead. It's worth upping your tea measurement and lowering the quantities of lemon and sugar with this method though.

PEACH ICED TEA

Preparation time: 5 minutes // Makes 1 glass

You might have had an artificial-tasting peach iced tea in a bottle that you bought from a petrol station for a long drive, but rest assured the real deal is worlds apart from that. Full-flavoured, sweet and ultra-refreshing, this will be a regular feature over your summer.

1 glass of Classic Iced Tea

15ml Monin peach syrup

1 slice of ripe peach

Mint sprigs

Ice

Fill your glass with loads of ice and then pour over the Classic Iced Tea, leaving room for the peach syrup. Add the peach syrup and watch it drizzle satisfyingly down through the drink, then give it a good stir. Garnish with the peach slice, a lovely sprig of fresh mint and a drinking straw.

Tips: Add a shot of vodka and half shot of crème de pêche for a dangerously downable, boozy refresher. Don't say we didn't warn you!

We use Monin peach syrup for this recipe, but it's not the easiest to come by in shops. You can get it from specialist hospitality retailers like Discount Cream Supplies (www.discountcream.co.uk) or you can find peach or apricot syrup in many international stores.

Peach Iced Tea

Classic Iced Tea

EARL GREY FRUIT CUP

Preparation time: 15 minutes, plus 1-2 hours cooling // Makes around 2 litres

This is the English summer in a cup: fruity, citrussy and sweet with a burst of berry flavour. Those frozen packs of berries from the supermarket are perfect for this; we always have them in the house to make smoothies with anyway. Alternatively, use your own selection of fresh berries.

10g loose leaf Earl Grey tea

1 litre boiling water

1 cup frozen summer fruit (or your choice of fresh summer berries)

Handful of fresh mint

1 litre apple juice

25ml elderflower cordial

To serve

Ice

Lemon slice

Mint sprig

First, make the tea and fruit infusion. Steep the tea in the freshly boiled water for 6-8 minutes, then strain it through a sieve into your serving vessel. Add the frozen fruit and fresh mint, then pop in the fridge until fully chilled.

Add the apple juice and elderflower cordial to the chilled tea and fruit infusion. Stir well, then serve over ice with a slice of lemon and a sprig of mint to garnish.

Tips

Give this fruit cup a garden party vibe by adding a shot of London dry gin to each glass and enjoy this drink in a whole new light!

MEET ME AT SUNRISE

Preparation time: 5 minutes, plus at least 4 hours infusing // Makes 1 litre

This recipe is from our good friend Sofie Vercauteren, aka 'Tearista' Sofie. We added white tea to her already delicious drink. Subtle and sweet, it's beautiful on a hot summer's day. See Meet Me At Sunset on page 61 for an alcoholic version of this infusion.

12g loose leaf Pai Mu Tan white tea (or any good quality white tea)

7-8 ripe strawberries, halved

2 star anise

1 litre cold water

To serve

Extra strawberries

Mint sprigs

Put the tea, strawberries and star anise into a jug or bottle and then add the cold water. Leave to infuse for 4 hours (minimum) or overnight in the fridge.

Strain the cold infusion into glasses over ice. To make a strawberry slice garnish, slice your strawberry top to bottom into 4-5mm slices then make a cut in the middle of the strawberry, from the bottom to about halfway up. You can then garnish the drink by sliding the strawberry over the edge of the glass. Looks proper classy. Add a sprig of mint to serve.

Tips

For the ultimate aperitif or dinner party welcome drink, try Meet Me At Sunset on page 61.

Meet Me
At Sunrise

Earl Grey
Fruit Cup

EARL GREY WHEAT IPA

Preparation time: 1 hour to brew, plus 5-7 days fermenting // Cooking time: 5-6 hours // Makes approximately 25 litres

For the malt

4kg crushed Maris Otter pale malt

3kg crushed wheat

1kg crushed Cara malt

1kg crushed Munich malt

For the bittering hops

25g Columbus

For the aroma

30g Amarillo hops

30g Simcoe hops

For the yeast

11g Munich Classic wheat beer yeast

For the dry hop

50g Amarillo hops

50g Simcoe hops

100g Earl Grey tea

Equipment

Mash tun with a false bottom or a fine muslin sack

Thermometer

Fermentation bucket

This recipe is for the home brewers out there. This is an all-grain recipe, so you will need a mash tun with a false bottom or a fine muslin sack to strain out the malt. You'll also need 17 to 20L of water at around 70°c to mash in your malt with, making sure you have no dry clumps. Following this, leave it in the mash container for 60 minutes.

At 60 minutes you can open the outlet for your false bottom or strain out the malt by hand, carefully pouring no more than 2L of water over it. This is called your sparge and by doing this you can collect any residual sugars from your mash.

Now you have your mash wort, you can start to heat this to a rolling boil. Once you have the rolling boil you can add your bittering hops.

From this point you want to keep it on a boil for 60 minutes. At the 60 minute mark you can take the heating element off and add your late aroma hops.

Leave this to stand for 10 minutes and then start cooling it down to a temperature between 17 and 20°c. You can use this point to add cold water to bring your beer down to the correct starting gravity and cool down your wort faster.

Now carefully pour your cooled wort into a clean and sanitised fermentation bucket, then pitch your packet of yeast directly in. Leave the container in a warm dry place to ferment. You'll want a small opening at the top through an airlock with water inside to allow the CO_2 to be released.

After 7 days, add your dry hops and the tea and then at day 10, strain off the beer and bottle or keg as you see fit. Store for 2 to 3 weeks to lightly carbonate.

ABBEYDALE BREWERY

We worked with Sheffield beer wizards, Abbeydale Brewery, on an incredible Earl Grey Wheat Beer and in the interests of enjoying tea in as many ways as possible, here is the recipe for the home brewers amongst you. Over to our brewer, Scott:

"The idea for this recipe came after trying a few similar styles from breweries like Marble Beers and Yeastie Boys. Inspiration led me to put together a nice malty wheat body and some citrussy, spicy rounded hops to balance out and complement the Earl Grey tea flavours. That's where Batch Tea Co. came in with their fantastic blend so I could finish my recipe off and set a date to start brewing."

ELDERFLOWER KOMBUCHA

Preparation time: 20 minutes, plus 7-14 days fermentation // Makes 8 x 250ml glasses

Kombucha is a phenomenal soft drink. Slightly sweet, slightly tangy, a little bit fizzy, and utterly delicious (when brewed properly!). Brewing with elderflower speeds up the fermentation process and creates the most refreshing drink. Be patient and keep trying, and feel free to contact Momo on Instagram for tips.

2 litres filtered water

120g raw cane sugar

3g black tea (we recommend Batch Tea Darjeeling 2nd flush)

11g green tea (we recommend Batch Tea Mao Feng)

3g dried elderflowers

400ml kombucha culture (aka the SCOBY – Symbiotic Culture of Bacteria & Yeast)

Equipment

Glass jar (minimum 3 litre)

Breathable cotton cloth to cover the jar

Rubber band to secure the cloth

First, brew the tea. Bring 500ml of the filtered water to the boil and pour into a jug. Stir in and dissolve all the sugar, then add the black tea. After about 2 minutes, when the water should have cooled to approximately 80-85°c, add the green tea and dried elderflowers. Steep for a further 10 minutes, then strain out the tea leaves and elderflowers.

Add the remaining 1.5 litres of filtered water to your jar and then add the sweet tea to cool it down. Now add the kombucha culture to the jar. This is the engine that drives the kombucha fermentation. Cover the jar with the breathable cloth. The purpose of this is to keep out flies and other nasties while allowing the kombucha to breathe, which is essential for fermentation.

Now you need to leave the covered jar in a clean, warm, environment. We'd recommend at least 21°c with the ideal temperature being approximately 28°c. After a few days you should see a white pellicle growing across the top; that is a good sign and tells you that the fermentation is working as it should. We would recommend that after about 7 days you taste the kombucha and see if it is to your liking, then keep trying every couple of days as it continues to ferment. Note: The majority of the sugar you added initially is consumed by the yeast during fermentation, so when you bottle the kombucha the sugar content should be low.

Now for the bottling and second fermentation. When you think the kombucha is ready, it is time to bottle it. Pour approximately 2 litres of the kombucha into bottles and tightly seal them. You now want to leave this for 3-7 days while it builds up carbonation. When there is a little fizz in the booch, pop the bottles in the fridge.

Having only bottled 2 litres of kombucha, you should have approximately 400ml left in the jar. Leave this in the jar with the newly formed pellicle and keep it covered with the breathable cloth. This kombucha will continue to ferment and should develop into a strong healthy starter liquid to use for your next batch.

MOMO

Momo Kombucha are Josh and Lisa: London-based purveyors of the finest organic certified kombucha around. With four delicious flavours, Ginger-Lemon; Turmeric; Elderflower; and Raspberry-Hibiscus, they're the perfect alcohol alternative. They brew every single batch the old-fashioned way in a small glass jar, which is the only way to produce the highest quality kombucha, and this is the way they'll always do it. Find them at www.momo-kombucha.com or @momokombucha on social media.

SPIRITS & COCKTAILS

Cocktails rock. Making them is loads of fun and great for parties. We all know that. But how do you make a cocktail really stand out?

Adding tea to cocktails entirely transforms them, bringing instant complexity to your drink's flavour profile to make basic alcohol and mixer combinations far more layered and sophisticated. A lot of mixologists like working with gin because of the varied flavour profiles in their bespoke selection of botanicals, and teas are no different in that respect.

Tea in cocktails is also a great talking point. If there's two things us Brits love, it's tea and booze: put them together and people usually smile. We know this first-hand from running our Tea Bar at events; a bit of booze tends to get people more excited about tea than us trying to describe our passion for it!

They're not only simple to use, but the tea-maker has already done most of the hard work for you. For example, a Lapsang Souchong instantly injects a bass note of old-world smokiness to a drink, further enhancing the peat of a whiskey or the pepper of a rye, and the rich bergamot of Earl Grey is being used more and more in martinis and Collins drinks.

Teas make great cocktail syrups too, which you can keep chilled and on-hand to add an extra dimension to any cocktail as and when you want to.

Finally, if you have friends and guests who don't drink, then teas are an absolute must for creating some truly amazing mocktails, graduating the drink from a boring mixture of fruit juices and soda bases to something far more delicate, considered and fun to drink.

There are infinite combinations for making "TeaTails" that you can try from two main approaches: tea as a mixer, or tea-infused spirits as the base for your cocktail. Or you could try both for a tea double whammy! We hope you love making the recipes in this chapter and more importantly, experimenting with your own creations to take your cocktail or mocktail game to the next level.

Big Red Mojito

Pornstar Mar-tea-ni

Brambearl

TEA-INFUSED SPIRITS

Infusing spirits with tea might sound like a complicated process but that couldn't be further from the truth. With the variety of teas available out there and the multitude of spirits to choose as your base, the options for creating new and exciting cocktails are endless. The only limit to your creativity is your imagination, and possibly your liver...

The basic premise of tea-infusing a spirit is this: Add around 24g of loose tea to 1 litre of your base spirit, then leave for up to 24 hours before straining. That's it. Yup. That really is it.

From there, you might find that your drink is perfect over ice, with tonic or you may want to craft the next great cocktail! Many of the cocktails in this book start with an infused spirit so it's a handy trick to get down and you'll be mixing up your own creations before long.

Here are a few staples that we use for cocktails and a couple of our favourites for sipping over ice or with tonic.

EARL GREY GIN

24g loose leaf Earl Grey tea

1 litre high-quality London dry gin

This is the base for a few cocktails in this book and creates a punchy flavour that stands up to some bold mixers. Use less tea for a lighter infusion that can be served over ice or with a light tonic such as Mediterranean, Indian or elderflower.

PHOENIX BLACK GIN

20g Dan Cong black tea

1 litre high-quality London dry gin

Perfect over ice or topped up with light Indian tonic and a slice of cucumber. Heaven.

Tips

Don't want to wait for your spirits to infuse? Use a cream whipper to infuse your spirits in less than 2 minutes! Simply add your tea leaves and spirit to the cream whipper, shake for 90 seconds, charge and pour through a strainer. This creates a lighter infusion that's perfect for sipping or enjoying with a light mixer.

MAO FENG VODKA

24g Mao Feng Green tea

1 litre high-quality vodka

Perfect over ice or with a light tonic. Alternatively, try it with cloudy apple juice and a dash of sugar syrup.

LAPSANG BOURBON

24g loose leaf Lapsang Souchong tea

1 litre high-quality bourbon (such as Bulleit)

Make the ultimate Old Fashioned with this smoky sweet treat.

BRAMBEARL

Makes 1 glass

Here's our fruitier than ever take on the classic Bramble cocktail. Earl Grey infused gin adds an orangey zing that pairs perfectly with cassis, lemon and blackberries for a wonderful short drink.

50ml Earl Grey gin (see page 58)

15ml sugar syrup

½ lemon, juiced

Ice cubes

Crushed ice

15ml crème de mure or crème de cassis

Soda

Mint sprig

2 fresh blackberries

Equipment

Boston or cocktail shaker

Rocks glass

2 short straws

Shake the tea-infused gin, sugar syrup and lemon juice with ice in the Boston or cocktail shaker. Fill the rocks glass with crushed ice, strain the gin mixture into the glass and then drizzle over the liqueur. Top up the glass with soda and then garnish with the mint, blackberries and straws.

BIG RED MOJITO

Makes 1 glass

This drink is named not for its colour but because it uses the wonderful Da Hong Pao (Big Red Robe) oolong tea for a sweet, slightly chocolatey, smooth edge to the classic crisp mojito. It's made just like a regular mojito but with Da Hong Pao infused white rum.

½ lime

Fresh mint

15ml sugar syrup

50ml Da Hong Pao white rum (infused at 24g per litre for up to 24 hours)

Crushed ice

Soda

Mint sprig

Wedge of lime

Equipment

Muddling spoon

355ml (12oz) hi-ball glass

2 straws

Muddle the lime, mint and sugar syrup in the bottom of your glass. Add the tea-infused rum and then fill the glass with crushed ice.
Top up the drink with soda, then garnish it with the mint sprig, wedge of lime and straws.

PORNSTAR MAR-TEA-NI

Preparation time: 5 minutes // Makes 2

Who doesn't love a Pornstar Martini? Our take elevates it slightly with a little extra fresh bitterness and even more tropical notes from the Dan Cong oolong tea. You won't be able to get enough! Passionfruit purée can be found online and everything else you should find in a supermarket.

Ice cubes

100ml Dan Cong vodka (infused at 25g per litre for 24 hours)

50ml Passoa passionfruit liqueur

25ml passionfruit purée (we use Monin, which you can easily find online. Don't substitute this with cordial, juice or pre-mixed cocktail drinks you find in supermarkets)

25ml lime juice

20ml vanilla syrup (again, we like Monin and you can find this in most supermarkets)

70ml Prosecco

1 fresh passionfruit, halved

Equipment

Boston or cocktail shaker

2 shot glasses

2 Prosecco or martini glasses

First, chill your glasses with ice cubes and cold water. Fill your shaker with ice cubes, add all the ingredients except the Prosecco and fresh passionfruit, then shake well for about 10 seconds.

Empty the chilled glasses and double strain the martini mixture evenly between them. Pop half a passionfruit, cut side upwards, into each drink and then fill your shot glasses with Prosecco to be served alongside the martini.

Tips

Substitute Dan Cong oolong tea with Dan Cong black tea to make a more mellow drink with a little more depth, although the finished martini will be slightly darker in colour.

MEET ME AT SUNSET

Preparation time: 5 minutes // Makes 1 flute

A deliciously light aperitif or welcome drink for a dinner party or event. Served in a champagne flute with a strawberry slice garnish, it looks the part and is super light, slightly sweet and gently sparkling.

1 strawberry slice garnish (see method)

80ml Meet Me At Sunrise cold infusion (see page 50)

Dash of Cointreau

80ml Prosecco

Dash of elderflower cordial

To make the strawberry slice garnish, slice a fresh strawberry from top to bottom into 4-5mm slices then make a cut in the middle of the strawberry, from the bottom to about halfway up. You can then garnish the drink by sliding the strawberry over the edge of the glass.

Pour the cold infusion into a chilled champagne flute, add the Cointreau then top up with Prosecco, leaving enough room for a splash of elderflower cordial. Give the drink a little stir and then finish it with your strawberry slice garnish.

SMOKY OLD FASHIONED

Makes 1 glass

Our tea-infused twist on this classic whisky cocktail adds lashings of smoky flavour with Lapsang Souchong and a good quality bourbon. Simply infuse 1 litre of your chosen whisky with 25g of Lapsang Souchong tea for 24 to 48 hours. It really packs the drink with a lovely 'woodfire' punch.

1 sugar cube (or 1 dessert spoon simple syrup)

Dash of bitters

50ml Lapsang Souchong whisky (see page 59)

1 large ice cube

1 orange

Equipment

Muddler

Stirrer

Whisky tumbler

Put the sugar cube or syrup into your tumbler and add a dash or two of bitters. Use the muddler to grind down the cube and mix the sugar with the bitters, then add the infused whisky and stir.

Add the ice cube and continue to stir the drink for 30 to 60 seconds. This allows the ingredients to meld and some of the ice to melt, softening and rounding out the flavours.

Peel a wide slice of zest from the orange, twist it to release the oils and then slide it down between the ice cube and the glass to serve.

SUMMER SYMPHONY

Preparation time: 5 minutes // Makes 2 glasses

Our very own cocktail and the one that started it all! Marc invented this for his wedding guests to enjoy on arrival, which sparked the whole Batch Tea Bar service. With Earl Grey gin, elderflower, lemon and mint, it's the perfect tipple for a warm summer's day.

Ice cubes

Bunch of fresh mint

100ml Earl Grey gin (see page 58)

30ml elderflower syrup

300ml diet bitter lemon

Mint sprigs, to garnish

Equipment

Boston or cocktail shaker

Tall glasses or gin glasses

Drinking straws

Half fill your cocktail shaker with ice and then tear in the bunch of mint. Pour over the gin and elderflower syrup, then shake vigorously for 10 seconds to infuse the liquid with fresh mint.

Fill two glasses with ice and strain the gin mixture into them, dividing it evenly. Top with the diet bitter lemon and then garnish with straws and mint sprigs to serve.

Meet Me At Sunset

Summer Symphony

Smoky Old Fashioned

EARL GREY GIN ICED TEA

Preparation time: 5 minutes, plus 30 minutes to cool the tea // Makes 4 glasses

Super light and refreshing short drink that packs a boozy gin punch for a summer's day! Lengthen as you wish or replace the Earl Grey with a straight up black tea for a less citrussy flavour.

4g loose leaf Earl Grey tea

350ml freshly boiled water

Ice

200ml London dry gin

1 lemon, juiced

60ml simple sugar syrup, or to taste (or add 4 tbsp sugar to the warm tea)

Lemon slices, to garnish

Steep your tea for 3 minutes in the freshly boiled water, then strain and allow to cool completely.

Add ice to 4 rocks or old fashioned glasses, then divide the ingredients equally between them in this order: gin first, then tea, lemon juice and sugar syrup to finish.

Garnish your iced tea with the lemon slices and serve.

CUCKOOSTONE DIY PHOENIX BLACK TEA GIN

Preparation time: 48 hours // Makes 70cl

Ade and Becky at the phenomenal artisan distillery Cuckoostone have created an unbelievable gin using Batch Tea Co. Phoenix Mountain Dan Cong Black Tea in their small batch distillation pot. As most of us don't have one of these at home, they've created a beautifully simple DIY version by infusing vodka with the tea and a selection of botanicals. Phoenix Black Tea Gin is made by imparting the flavour of the tea at distillation rather than infusing afterwards, undergoing a process called vapour infusion, which is what takes place in the still pot. This works by heating the grain spirit to a vapour that passes through the botanicals, which are hung in a fine mesh bag inside the still, to impart their flavour. The flavoured vapour is then cooled to a liquid state. As the botanicals are not steeped in the spirit directly, they are less affected by heat, resulting in perfectly balanced flavours and a deliciously smooth end product.

2g Phoenix Black Tea

2 tbsp juniper berries

1-2 black peppercorns

1 tsp coriander seeds

1 tsp fennel seeds

½ cinnamon stick

700ml good quality neutral vodka

0.5g unwaxed lemon peel, white pith removed

0.5g unwaxed orange peel, white pith removed

Put the loose tea and botanicals, minus the peel, into a sterilised heatproof jar or glass bottle, then top with the vodka and leave to infuse for 24 hours in a cool dark place.

After 24 hours, have a quick taste and then add the fresh peel. Leave for another 12-24 hours, tasting occasionally to make sure you're not over-steeping the liquor, and shake the jar once or twice to give the botanicals a nudge.

Once you're happy with the flavour, strain the gin through a fine sieve or filter and leave for a couple more days. Filter again if desired, then serve over ice with a good quality tonic and enjoy!

Earl Grey Gin
Iced Tea

LONG ISLAND ICED TEA

Preparation time: 5 minutes // Makes 4 glasses

The most famous tea to contain no tea! Until we came along. Knock your socks off with our take on a classic. Refreshing but not for the faint of heart. You'll want your classic iced tea mix to be strong and sweeter than usual to mimic the sugary cola it's replacing.

Ice cubes

50ml vodka

50ml white rum

50ml silver tequila

50ml London dry gin

50ml Cointreau

50ml lemon juice

50ml rich simple syrup (2 parts sugar to 1 part water)

400ml classic iced tea, brewed extra strong and sweet (see page 48)

Lemon slices, to garnish

Mint sprigs, to garnish

Equipment

Cocktail shaker (although you can get by without)

Half fill the cocktail shaker with ice, then add the spirits, Cointreau, lemon juice and simple syrup. Give it a good shake for 10 seconds. Fill your glasses with fresh ice and divide the shaken mixture evenly between them. Top up with the iced tea, add straws and garnish with the lemon and mint. It's probably best not to enjoy too many...

SPICED PEACH ICED TEA

Preparation time: 5 minutes // Makes 145ml

Complex but still fresh, the complexity of tea is in perfect harmony with the spice of the rum here. This has a peachy twist but most stone or citrus fruits would work too.

50ml Cane Toad Khanage Wars Spiced Rum

50ml cold strong tea

25ml crème de peche

10ml lemon juice

10ml sugar syrup

Peach or nectarine slices, to garnish

Build the ingredients over ice in a highball glass and garnish with slices of fresh peach or nectarine. We use loose leaf Tie Guan Yin oolong (translated as Iron Goddess of Mercy) but the cocktail works with any of the lighter blends of tea.

ZYMURGORIUM

Zymurgorium are an epic Manchester-based brewery and distillery, who regularly knock out incredible craft beers, mead, never seen before gins and a range of other exciting spirits. Creative as anything you've ever seen, they're pioneers in an already innovative industry. Find Zymurgorium at www.zymurgorium.com or @zymurgorium on social media and in real life at the stunning Project Halcyon bar at Manchester Studios.

Spiced Peach Iced Tea

Long Island
Iced Tea

UNFORESEEABLE CHAI COCKTAIL

Preparation time: 5 minutes, plus 20-30 minutes cooling time // Makes 1 6oz glass

The best dirty chai you'll ever try. Gina from the incredible Saw Grinders Union in Sheffield came up with this little beauty after falling in love with Kama Sutra Sticky Chai and just having to create something beautiful with it.

50ml oat milk infused with Kama Sutra Sticky Chai (see method)

35ml Ancho Reyes chilli liqueur

20ml Mozart dark chocolate liqueur

20ml Kahlua

2 dashes of chocolate and chilli bitters

Ice

Equipment

Boston shaker

Strainer

Hurricane glass

For the chai infused oat milk, stir 20g (about 4 teaspoons) of Kama Sutra Sticky Chai into 150ml of heated oat milk. Let it brew for about 20 minutes and allow to cool. The longer you let it sit, the more intense the chai flavour. This makes enough for roughly 3 cocktails.

For the cocktail, combine all the ingredients in a Boston shaker and add ice. Give it a good shake and then discard the ice. Now dry shake the mixture, hard! This will give the drink a nice creamy head once poured. Double strain the cocktail into a fluted glass and garnish with dried chai to serve.

Tips

Feel free to use whatever milk or plant-based alternative you have. We just find that oat milk creates the best creaminess!

While some of these ingredients might not be available from your average supermarket, they're easily available online.

SAW GRINDERS UNION

Saw Grinders Union is a leading light in the resurgence of Sheffield's Industrial Quarter. Outstanding cocktails from consummate professionals in mixology, set in a beautiful space in one of Sheffield's most iconic industrial-era buildings, plus incredible coffee, beer, cocktails, and burgers. Find them at www.sawgrindersunion.com or @ saw.grinders.union on social media.

ON THE PLATE

As we focused on in the previous section, people tend to associate tea with a hot or cold drink in a cup, yet it has been used in a much wider variety of recipes around the world for a long time. Tea can be a flavour enhancer and/or garnish in both savoury and sweet dishes: black tea adds depth to hearty stews, green tea brings vibrancy and freshness, oolong can work as a great natural sweetener and Earl Grey is well suited to baking with, though it's by no means the only tea you can add to cakes, biscuits, breads and more. If you're thinking that cooking with tea seems like a gimmick, consider the health benefits we outlined earlier (especially if you're consuming the whole leaf) and that it can be a great way to reuse tea leaves. Tea is basically a herb and can be used as such, so cooking with the liquor, the leaf (ground, whole, chopped) or both creates different effects for different dishes.

One of our wonderful customers, Jeremy Pemberton, sent us this brilliant tip about cooking with tea instead of alcohol in food:

"Most of us imagine that when there is alcohol in food, the alcohol simply 'cooks off'. It does, but only after a great deal more cooking than the majority of people will give their food. For most, this is not a problem. However, for those intolerant to alcohol, recovering alcoholics, or even those cooking for children, what can be done? Do you just avoid all those recipes that demand a slug of sherry or brandy, or half a bottle of white wine? What about the Christmas cake? You could simply omit those ingredients… but you don't need to sacrifice all that extra flavour. Instead, use tea. Substitute the alcohol that the recipe demands for your favourite tea flavours. Hot or cold, any variety or blend you like. Experiment. Make extra strong Lapsang Souchong for casseroles. Earl Grey works well in cakes, or in a risotto instead of vermouth. Soak your dried fruit in a cold fragrant tea overnight for fruit cakes that pop with flavour and moisture. Tea is amazingly versatile, making your alcohol-free cooking just as delicious, and good for absolutely everyone to enjoy. Tea is the answer!"

BREAKFAST

Tea is synonymous with breakfast in this country. There's nothing quite like a steaming hot mug of tea to wake you up in the morning. But why stop there when you could add it to your eggs, smoothies, overnight oats and even pancakes?

FLUFFY GLUTEN-FREE TEA PANCAKES

Preparation time: 55 minutes // Cooking time: less than 5 minutes // Serves 4

Infusing milk with tea is a great way to add extra flavour to deliciously fluffy pancakes that partner with a variety of toppings like compotes, syrups and crispy bacon. This recipe uses Earl Grey but is equally great with chai or even a malty breakfast tea. If you're fine with gluten, simply use regular self-raising flour and omit the xanthan gum.

200ml milk of your choice

10g loose leaf Earl Grey tea or 4 Earl Grey teabags (if using chai or breakfast tea, we recommend 20g or 8 teabags)

200g gluten-free self-raising flour

1 tbsp caster sugar

1 tsp baking powder

½ tsp xanthan gum

Pinch of salt

2 eggs

50g butter

Heat the milk in a saucepan until you start to see small bubbles and then add the tea. Stir and leave to cool until the milk is at room temperature.

In a large mixing bowl, combine the flour, sugar, baking powder, xanthan gum and salt. Make a well in the flour, break in the eggs and mix with the dry ingredients. Strain the infused milk into the bowl and whisk to incorporate everything until you have a smooth batter.

Melt the butter in a frying pan and leave to cool a little before stirring it into the batter, then leave it to rest for 5 to 10 minutes. This just allows time for the baking powder to give the batter a little lift for extra-light, fluffy pancakes. Give the pan a little wipe to remove excess butter if needed but you can use what's left to fry the first pancakes in!

Put the frying pan back on a medium heat and steadily pour one small ladle of mixture into the pan, creating a circular pancake about 7.5cm (3 inches) in diameter. Cook on one side until bubbles start to appear on the top (roughly 2 minutes) before flipping to cook the other side for a further minute.

Repeat with the remaining batter. The pancakes should be golden brown, light and airy.

We love these Earl Grey pancakes with fresh strawberries, whipping cream and fresh mint leaves.

Try different combinations of tea pancakes with tea and fruit compotes (see page 146) or streaky bacon and maple syrup/tea-infused syrups (see page 144).

FRUITY TEA SMOOTHIES

Preparation time: 5 minutes // Makes 2 glasses

Get your morning cup of tea and breakfast in one glass by adding tea to a smoothie for a hit of fruit, protein, caffeine and antioxidants that tastes great. Below are a few of our favourites but do experiment with your own combinations: there are so many fruits, teas, herbs, flavourings and even vegetables to choose from!

EARL GREY & BLUEBERRY SMOOTHIE

5g loose leaf Earl Grey tea

100ml freshly boiled water

1 banana

100g frozen blueberries

25g oats

10 basil leaves

2 tbsp Greek or plant-based yoghurt

1 tbsp honey or plant-based syrup

1 tbsp lemon juice

To make any of these smoothies, simply steep the tea in the freshly boiled or 80°c water and then add all the ingredients – including the wet tea leaves – to a blender and blitz until smooth. Enjoy!

FOREST FRUITS & DIANHONG BLACK TEA SMOOTHIE

5g loose leaf Dianhong black tea

60ml freshly boiled water

1 banana

100g frozen forest fruits

30ml apple juice

25g oats

6 fresh mint leaves

2 tbsp Greek or plant-based yoghurt

1 tbsp honey or plant-based syrup

MANGO & GREEN TEA SMOOTHIE

5g loose leaf Mao Feng or Longjing green tea

100ml water at 80°c

100g frozen mango, or 1 large fresh mango

50ml milk of your choice

10 fresh basil leaves

3 tbsp Greek or plant-based yoghurt

1 tbsp honey or plant-based syrup

Forest Fruits & Dianhong Black Tea Smoothie

Mango & Green Tea Smoothie

Earl Grey & Blueberry Smoothie

GREEN TEA SCRAMBLED EGGS

Preparation time: 5 minutes // Cooking time: 5 minutes // Serves 1-2

This one's a tip from Owen's Tea Master instructor back in Australia: to add an extra healthy kick to your scrambled eggs in the morning, throw in some green tea leaves before serving. I like to use something with a punchy but not overpowering flavour like sencha or mao feng.

2-3g loose leaf green tea

1 tsp butter

3 eggs

Splash of water

Brew the tea and save the leaves. Drink the tea.

Add the butter to a non-stick frying pan on a medium heat.

Whisk the eggs and water together, then add them to the pan.

Once the eggs are cooked to your liking, turn off the heat and fold in the rehydrated green tea leaves.

Serve piping hot and enjoy.

MATCHA OVERNIGHT OATS

Preparation time: 5 minutes, plus overnight in the fridge // Serves 2

This easy breakfast option has become a staple for the health-conscious foodie. Matcha adds an antioxidant and caffeine boost to your morning and, of course, delicious flavour. You can make overnight oats with just about anything, so try your own combinations of nuts, berries, seeds or nutritional supplements to add extra flavour, protein and nutrition.

150ml milk of your choice

100g Greek or plant-based yoghurt

100g frozen berries

50g good quality jumbo oats

1 tbsp honey or plant-based syrup

2 tsp chia seeds (optional)

2 tsp organic matcha

Add all the ingredients to a container or bowl and stir well to mix everything together. Cover and leave in the fridge overnight.

When you're ready to eat, remove the overnight oats from the fridge and check whether they need a little extra liquid to get the right consistency. Garnish with fresh berries, banana slices, granola, a drizzle of honey, syrup or whatever you like!

Tips: Avoid using cheap flaky porridge oats as these will end up a little mushy. Jumbo oats will leave a little texture and be much more enjoyable! Overnight oats will last for a few days in the fridge, so you can make a batch for the week to make breakfast even easier.

LIGHT TEA SYRUP WITH FRESH FRUIT

Preparation time: 5 minutes, plus 20-30 minutes cooling // Cooking time: 5 minutes // Serves 2

This dish works beautifully at breakfast, as a light snack or even after dinner. It looks divine and is a delicious combination of melon, peach, juicy berries and sweet syrup, which is broadly the same as our other tea syrups (see page 144) but not reduced for a lighter finish.

10g loose leaf Mao Feng green tea (but feel free to experiment with other teas!)

225ml water

200g sugar

1 ripe peach

6-8 melon balls (or about ¼ honeydew or cantaloupe melon)

Handful each of raspberries, strawberries and blueberries

2 tbsp high protein natural yoghurt (optional)

Mint sprigs, to garnish

Using a filter in a cup or jar, steep the tea in 225ml of water at a temperature according to the regular preparation technique (i.e. 80°c for green tea, 100°c for black tea, etc.) for 3 minutes.

Strain the infusion, then add the sugar and stir until dissolved. Chill the syrup in the fridge, or to cool it more quickly transfer the syrup to a pan and stir, then pop the pan into a bowl of ice.

Meanwhile, dice the peach and use a melon-baller to make the melon balls, or just chop the melon into 2.5cm cubes. Layer the fresh fruit (melon, peach and fresh berries) in glasses or bowls.

Pour over the cooled tea syrup, add a dollop of yoghurt to each bowl (if using) and then garnish with the fresh mint to serve.

Tips

Teas with sweet and savoury notes work well in this syrup, such as Sejak, Dong Ding oolong or malty Chinese black teas.

MAINS

From bringing out extra flavours to adding health benefits, using tea in your savoury dishes might just be a revelation, but it's a practice that is as commonplace as eating bread in some cultures.

In this chapter you'll find a selection of fish, meat and vegetarian main meals that use poaching, roasting, braising and even smoking to infuse ingredients with the wonderful flavours of various complementary teas.

Happy cooking!

FRAGRANT TEA-
BRAISED BEEF

Preparation time: 20 minutes // Cooking time: 2 hours (or 6 hours in a slow cooker) // Serves 4

A Chinese style claypot dish, perfect with rice and Chinese vegetables on a cold evening. Cook in a casserole and transfer to the oven or use a slow cooker. We add a little spice and zing which contrasts beautifully with the rich, thick gravy.

10g loose leaf Yunnan black tea (or any strong malty black tea)

600ml freshly boiled water

1 beef stock pot

3 tbsp rapeseed oil

2 dried red chillies (optional)

1 tsp Sichuan peppercorns (optional)

3cm root ginger, grated

6 cloves of garlic, sliced

6 spring onions, thinly sliced

1kg braising beef, cubed

2 tbsp plain flour

4 cloves

1 bay leaf

2 star anise

2 fresh red chillies, one halved lengthways, the other sliced widthways

2 green peppers, sliced

1 tsp Chinese five spice

2 tbsp Shaoxing rice wine

3 tbsp light soy sauce

2 tbsp dark soy sauce

1 tbsp rice vinegar

1 tbsp sugar

1 tsp toasted sesame oil

Sprig of fresh coriander, to garnish

Steep your tea leaves in the freshly boiled water for 5 minutes, then strain and stir the stock pot into the tea liquor. Preheat your oven to 150°c.

Heat half of the oil in a heavy-based casserole on a medium-high heat, then add the dried chillies and Sichuan peppercorns, if using, to fry until fragrant, being careful not to burn the chilli. Remove with a slotted spoon, then fry the ginger, garlic and spring onions in the remaining oil until fragrant before transferring them to a plate.

Toss the beef chunks in the flour and brown on all sides in the hot casserole using another tablespoon of oil (depending on the size of your pot this might take a few batches, as you don't want to overcrowd it) and then rest the seared beef on a plate.

Heat the remaining oil and fry the cloves, bay leaf, star anise and the halved fresh chilli until fragrant, then add the green peppers and stir fry for a minute. Put the beef back into the pot with the five spice and aromatics, then stir to coat the meat well.

Pour in the rice wine and stir to deglaze the pan, then add the soy sauces, vinegar, sugar and sesame oil. Finally, pour in your tea stock, stir to mix everything together, then cover the pot and transfer to the oven for 1 hour 30 minutes to 2 hours, until the meat is tender and falls apart. Stir once or twice throughout and check that the sauce isn't drying up too much. If you're using a slow cooker, put it on a high heat for around 6 hours, stirring once or twice during that time.

Season to taste with salt and serve in a bowl with long grain or brown rice and braised pak choi. Garnish with the sliced red chilli and a sprig of fresh coriander.

GREEN TEA POACHED SALMON

Preparation time: 15 minutes, plus 1 hour cooling // Serves 12 (as part of a spread)

Dinner or garden party on the horizon? Serve up this extremely simple centrepiece to wow your guests! For a family meal, use salmon fillets instead and serve with noodles or rice and salad.

60g soft light brown sugar

2 lemons, sliced

100g loose leaf green tea such as Bi Luo Chun, Mao Feng or Sejak

1 side of salmon (about 1kg)

To serve

Salad leaves

Spring onions

Pomegranate seeds

1 lemon, cut into wedges

Bring 4 litres of water to the boil in a pan and then turn off the heat. Add the sugar and sliced lemons while it cools. After about 6 minutes, stir in the tea leaves and allow to steep for about 5 minutes. Remove the tea leaves and then strain the poaching liquid into a roasting tin large enough to hold the whole side of salmon.

Place the tin on a medium-high heat and bring the poaching liquid back to the boil. Carefully submerge the salmon, skin side down. Let it simmer for a minute or so, then turn off the heat and allow to cool completely.

Once cooled, transfer the poached salmon to a flat board, cover with another board or plate and flip the whole thing carefully to turn the salmon over. Peel away any skin before moving the salmon onto a serving platter. Garnish with the salad leaves, spring onions, pomegranate seeds and enough lemon wedges for everyone to squeeze over their portion. You could also serve this with the green tea sauce on page 135.

INDIAN SPICED MUSHROOM AND ASSAM BROTH

Preparation time: 10 minutes // Cooking time: 60-90 minutes // Serves 2-4

A simple, playful vegan twist on a mushroom consommé crossed with an Asian-style soup. Indian spices, sweet nutty almond and a bitter caramel maltiness from the Assam tea mingle with deep earthy mushroom flavours, creating a rich and moreish broth while entertaining the taste buds!

1 tbsp fresh thyme leaves

50g blanched almonds

50g dried porcini mushrooms

2-3 tbsp vegetable oil

1 tsp each cumin, fennel and mustard seeds

2 shallots, finely diced

1 carrot, finely diced

1 stick of celery, finely diced

3 mushroom stock cubes

1500ml boiling water

2 Assam teabags

1 tbsp each fresh minced ginger, garlic and chilli

150g shiitake mushrooms, sliced

150g button mushrooms, sliced

1 tsp each ground cumin and coriander

100g dairy-free butter

100ml almond milk

Bunch of fresh coriander, chopped

Blitz or finely chop the thyme and almonds, then lightly toast in a dry frying pan with the porcini mushrooms.

In a medium-size pan, bring the oil to a medium heat and then add the cumin, fennel and mustard seeds. Fry for 1-2 minutes, stirring often to ensure they don't burn, then add the shallot, carrot and celery. Cook this mixture for 5-10 minutes until soft and translucent.

Meanwhile, dissolve the mushroom stock cubes in the boiling water (a large jug is best for this) and then add the teabags. Leave to brew for about 5 minutes before removing the teabags.

Stir the ginger, garlic and chilli into the softened vegetables and cook for 5 minutes, then add the sliced shiitake and button mushrooms. Stir in the ground cumin and coriander while they cook down for about 10 minutes.

Add the dairy-free butter to the pan along with the toasted almond mixture. Combine this with the mushroom base before turning up the heat and stirring in the almond milk. Continue cooking until the liquid has almost reduced to nothing, then turn the heat down low and pour in the Assam-infused mushroom stock. Leave the broth to cook on the lowest heat possible, with a lid on the pan, for up to an hour. Stir and taste occasionally, adding any seasoning you think it needs.

Pour the finished broth through a fine sieve into a clean pan to remove the solids. Your broth is now ready to be served and garnished with fresh coriander.

Tips

If like me you loathe food waste, make these mini mushroom pakora with the leftovers! Combine the drained and cooled mushrooms from the broth with gram flour at a 2:1 ratio along with 2 tablespoons of ground turmeric, 1 tablespoon of chilli powder and the remaining fresh coriander. Shape the mixture into discs and shallow fry in oil for 1-2 minutes on a medium heat.

THE BHAJI SHOP

The Bhaji Shop is one of our favourite cafés not only in Sheffield but in the world! Based in Sheffield city centre's Hideaway, it's something to behold and serves up beautiful freshly made curries, street food and onion bhajis. We love to while away the hours there imagining we're still backpackers, watching folks go by. Hosted by the wonderful Anna and Matt, you're in for a treat. Find them @thebhajishop on Facebook or Instagram.

PUNJABI CHOLE MASALA

Preparation time: 15 minutes or overnight // Cooking time: 25-30 minutes (more in pressure cooker) // Serves 3-4

We worked with our friend and fantastic cook, Seena Devaki, to create this authentic, tasty tea recipe. Chole masala, or chana masala, is ubiquitous as a street food dish right across India. Simple, rich, delicious and healthy, it's a store-cupboard staple worthy of any home. Strong black tea adds depth and richness. Traditionally, dried chickpeas are soaked overnight and then cooked in a pressure cooker with tea to absorb the colour, flavour and tannin tartness but you can also use tinned chickpeas for a quicker meal (we've provided both methods below).

For the pressure cooker method

250g dried chickpeas

½ bay leaf

1 small cinnamon stick

2 black teabags

Pinch of salt

For the tinned chickpea method

2 x 400g tins of cooked chickpeas

100ml strong black tea liquor

For both methods

2 tbsp vegetable oil

1 tsp cumin seeds

2.5cm fresh ginger, crushed

5 cloves of garlic, crushed

2 medium onions, chopped

1 tomato, chopped

½ tsp Kashmiri chilli powder

½ tsp garam masala powder

Pinch of turmeric (optional)

Pinch of black salt

Drizzle of honey

Fresh coriander leaves, chopped

2 green chillies, slit lengthways

Fresh ginger, julienned (optional)

For the pressure cooker method

Soak the dried chickpeas overnight in enough water to just cover them. The next day, pour the soaked chickpeas and water into a pressure cooker with the bay leaf, cinnamon stick, teabags and salt to taste. Allow three whistles of the pressure cooker to cook the chickpeas.

For both methods

Heat the oil in a large pan before adding the cumin seeds, then when they start to splutter stir in the crushed ginger and garlic. Sauté the mixture, add the chopped onions and continue to sauté until softened. Add the chopped tomato, then when the oil begins to separate stir in the Kashmiri chilli powder, garam masala and pinch of turmeric if using.

Now either remove the teabags, bay leaf and cinnamon stick from the pressure-cooked chickpeas and transfer them to the spiced onion mixture, including the water they were cooked in, or simply drain and rinse the tinned chickpeas, then add them to the spiced onion mixture along with the tea liquor. Season the chole masala with black salt to taste and allow to simmer for a few minutes.

Add a drizzle of honey to taste and then garnish the chole masala with the chopped coriander, green chillies and julienned ginger (if using) to serve.

TEA ROASTED CHICKEN LEGS

Preparation time: 30 minutes, plus at least 2 hours marinating // Cooking time: 40-45 minutes // Serves 4

Marinating chicken in a tea-based marinade overnight adds a beautiful rich aroma to the meat, which can then be served as a hearty winter dish with roasted vegetables or with chilled summery accompaniments like quinoa or bulgur wheat salad and leafy garnish. We like to use green tea or a roasted tea like hojicha for extra depth.

1 tbsp loose leaf tea

240ml hot water

1 tbsp dried rosemary

2 tsp salt

1 tsp mustard seeds

1 tsp dried thyme

1 tsp freshly ground black pepper

2 tbsp honey

4 skin-on, bone-in chicken legs

First, brew the tea leaves in the hot water and then leave to cool to room temperature. Meanwhile, combine the rosemary, salt, mustard seeds, thyme and pepper in a large zip-lock or sealable freezer bag. Stir the honey into the cooled tea and then add it to the herby mix in the bag.

Put the chicken legs into the bag and rub the tea mixture all over them, working it into the skin and any creases. Pop the bag into the fridge and leave to marinate for at least 2 hours, or overnight.

Remove the chicken from the fridge about 15-20 minutes before you want to start cooking and preheat your oven to 210°c. Empty the bags into an ovenproof dish and roast the chicken legs for around 40-45 minutes, or until the juices in the thickest part of the leg run clear. The skin should be crispy and golden brown and the chicken tender and juicy.

Serve with black tea infused bulgur wheat and roasted cherry tomato salad (see page 136) and dressed green leaves.

TEA SMOKED FISH

Preparation time: 10 minutes // Cooking time: 20-30 minutes // Serves 4

For the less adventurous cooks among us, the idea of smoking foods might seem a step too far. However, it really is a lot easier than it sounds and you certainly don't need a swanky smoking kettle to try this in the comfort of your own home. As the smoking is all happening in its own little foil tent, not much of the smoke escapes (no more than when searing a steak). Once you've given it a go with this recipe, you'll see how quick and easy making smoked food is and can get creative with all sorts of things from chicken to cheese.

50g long grain rice

50g pure cane sugar

20g loose leaf tea of your choice

Dried spices like cinnamon or star anise (optional)

4 fillets of fish (any fish really but salmon, trout and mackerel work really well or you could try something like octopus!)

You can do this on the hob, barbecue or even a campfire. Needless to say, it's easier to regulate the temperature on a hob so if you're using a barbecue or open fire, make sure you get nice white embers to cook on. Go and get creative!

Line a wok or deep roasting tin with foil so that it overhangs the edge by a few centimetres. Add your smoking ingredients (that's everything except the fish!) and make sure they're well mixed. If you're using teabags rather than loose leaf, empty the tea leaves out and discard the bags themselves. There are so many teas to choose from but we recommend trying greens and blacks, or to double down on the smoky flavour, lapsang souchong works a treat. Ideally, place a wire rack inside the wok or roasting tin that sits about 2cm above the smoking ingredients, but if you don't have one that fits, covering the tea mixture with tin foil will do the job.

Place the wok or tin over a medium heat and wait until a little smoke starts to show. This should take about 5 minutes. Lay the fish on the wire rack or foil, then cover the whole thing with another layer of foil. Crimp the top and bottom layers of foil together along the edges, ensuring there's some space over the top of the fish so that the smoke can circulate properly.

Turn the heat down low and leave for around 20 minutes until the fish is cooked. Serve with your favourite sides and enjoy.

Tips

You can also cold-smoke different foods using this method. Get the ingredients smoking and then turn off the heat. You'll need to give it another blast of heat for a minute or so every 10 minutes to produce more smoke.

If you're smoking something like chicken or pork, it's worth finishing off in the oven to make sure it's fully cooked. If you're unsure, you can always check the internal heat of your food using a cooking thermometer to confirm.

TEA SMOKED SALMON FILLETS WITH PAK CHOI AND JASMINE RICE

Preparation time: 20 minutes, plus 1 hour curing // Cooking time: 25 minutes // Serves 4

This might sound fancy but is actually quite simple and will wow your family, guests, anyone really! Smoking with tea adds a beautiful fragrance that infuses your food with a soft, smoky flavour and delicious aroma. Experiment with different teas for different experiences, or for different proteins. We like to use simple recipes or marinades to let the tea really shine through.

1 tsp Chinese five spice

1 tsp sea salt

½ tsp raw sugar (regular sugar works fine too)

4 salmon fillets (ideally all an even thickness)

25-30g Chinese loose leaf black tea

4 tbsp long grain rice

2 tbsp brown sugar

300g jasmine rice

1 tbsp vegetable oil

1 tsp minced garlic

1 tsp grated ginger

6-8 pak choi

1 tsp dark soy sauce

1 tbsp light soy sauce

1 tsp white rice vinegar

1 tsp toasted sesame oil

2 tsp toasted sesame seeds

2 spring onions, thinly sliced

Laoganma crispy chilli oil, to garnish (optional)

Mix the five spice with the sea salt and sugar, then rub this mixture into the salmon fillets until coated. Leave them in the fridge for an hour or so to cure. Half an hour before you want to start cooking, take the salmon out and let it return to room temperature. The fish should feel tacky on the surface; this means the smoke will stick and result in a great flavour.

Line a large wok or roasting tin with 2 layers of tin foil about 20cm across. Combine the Chinese tea, long grain rice and brown sugar and spread the mixture evenly over the foil. Place a steamer basket on top so the centre sits a few centimetres above the smoking ingredients, allowing space for the smoke to circulate.

Place the wok or tin over a high heat for 3-4 minutes until you begin to see a little smoke escaping. While the wok is heating up, put the jasmine rice on to cook. When smoke appears, place the cured salmon in the steamer basket with space between the fillets so they aren't touching each other or the sides. Cover the wok or tin with foil or a tight-fitting lid.

Reduce the heat to low and cook for around 8 minutes, depending on preference (we like ours done medium). For delicious caramelisation on top of the salmon, you can then quickly grill the fillets for a minute or so under a high heat, being careful not to overcook them. Set aside in a slightly warm oven to rest.

While the salmon is resting, quickly (and carefully) transfer the foil lining and smoking mixture to an ash-proof bin, then add the vegetable oil to the wok and turn the heat up to medium-high. When hot, add the garlic and ginger, stir-fry until fragrant, then add the pak choi and stir-fry for 2-3 minutes, or until tender. Add the soy sauces and vinegar to the wok and continue to cook for a further minute, or until heated through.

Remove the pan from the heat, drizzle the pak choi with sesame oil and serve over the jasmine rice in bowls. Place a salmon fillet in each bowl on top, then sprinkle over the sesame seeds and sliced spring onions. We like to add a dollop of crispy chilli oil to the bowls for a fragrant, spicy kick.

Tips: This recipe works beautifully with firm tofu too! Simply cut the tofu into approximately 0.75cm slices and increase the smoking time to anywhere from 10 to 20 minutes, depending on how smoky you like it. You can then stir-fry the tofu in a little oil to get nice crispy edges.

TEA-BONE STEAK

Preparation time: 45 minutes // Cooking time: 25 minutes // Serves 4

A classic British dish with a tea twist! The T-bone steak is encrusted with salt, pepper and tea to be served alongside Earl Grey confit tomatoes and Earl Grey salted twice-cooked chips. This recipe from chef Luke Rhodes, of MasterChef: The Professionals, includes tea in each element, beautifully complementing the dish without overpowering its flavours.

For the steak au poivre

4 T-bone steaks

15g loose leaf Lapsang Souchong tea

20g coarsely ground black pepper

20g Maldon sea salt

25g garlic powder

250g butter

200ml double cream

For the confit tomatoes

250ml garlic-infused olive oil

4 salad tomatoes

100g loose leaf Earl Grey tea

For the twice-cooked chips

4 large russet baking potatoes

1 litre vegetable oil

2 tsp Earl Grey tea salt (see page 137)

For the steak au poivre

Leave your T-bone steaks out of the fridge for a minimum of 1 hour before cooking to allow them to reach room temperature. To make the crust, mix the tea, black pepper, sea salt and garlic powder together in a bowl and set aside.

For the confit tomatoes

Pour the garlic oil into a saucepan and place over a low heat. Cut your tomatoes in half and place them into the oil, making sure they are submerged. Stir in the Earl Grey and cook for 20 minutes on a low heat.

For the twice-cooked chips

Cut the potatoes into chip shapes and cook them in boiling salted water for 8-10 minutes. Remove them from the pan and let them cool completely. Heat the vegetable oil to 180°c in a fryer, or deep pan, to get ready for the second cooking stage.

For the steak au poivre

While the oil for the chips is heating up, pat the steaks dry and then season heavily with the pepper crust. Preheat a griddle or heavy-based frying pan until it sizzles when you add a drop of oil. For a medium-rare interior, sear the steaks over a high heat for 5 to 6 minutes on each side. Only turn them once a rich, golden crust has formed and then reduce the heat slightly. 30 seconds before removing the steaks from the pan, add the butter and baste them as it melts. When cooked to your liking, remove the steaks from the pan and leave them to rest for 8 minutes, turning them over after half the time.

Add the cream to the still-hot pan to emulsify all the butter and turn all those meaty juices into a delicious pan-sauce to serve with the steak.

While the steak is resting, fry your chips in the hot oil for 7 minutes until they're nice and crisp, and then season with Earl Grey tea salt. Serve the rested steaks with the confit tomatoes, twice-cooked chips and creamy pan-sauce. You could also add our Earl Grey carrots on page 136. Enjoy!

LUKE RHODES

Luke Rhodes is one of Sheffield's best known chefs, made even more famous after becoming a MasterChef: The Professionals 2020 Quarter Finalist for his hearty, bold British cuisine. Luke is now chef director at the outstanding Chef Luke Rhodes private dining. Find Luke at @cheflukerhodes on social media.

YUNNAN BLACK TEA POACHED CHICKEN WITH HOJICHA RICE

Preparation time: 30 minutes // Cooking time: 20 minutes // Serves 4

This is a beautifully light summer dish that can also be given an autumnal twist with tea-infused pearl barley and roasted vegetables instead of the rice and salad. Try using green tea in the poaching liquor for an equally delicious take on this dish.

2 tbsp sesame seeds

2 star anise

60g light brown sugar

Pinch of salt

10g Yunnan black tea (or other malty black tea)

4 chicken breast fillets (or use legs for a really juicy end result)

265g jasmine or long grain rice

5g hojicha

1 tsp rice wine

1 tsp rice vinegar

2 tsp toasted sesame oil

3 tbsp light soy sauce

To serve

Fresh salad leaves

1 bunch of asparagus or other seasonal greens, lightly cooked

2 spring onions, sliced

Toast the sesame seeds in a warm heavy based pan, then transfer to a bowl and leave to cool. Bring 2 litres of water to the boil with the star anise and 30g of the brown sugar mixed in. Turn off the heat, season with salt, add your tea leaves and then set aside for about 10 minutes to allow the tea to infuse.

Once infused, strain the poaching liquor and then bring it back to the boil before reducing the heat to low. Let the liquid cool to room temperature before adding the chicken, as this will prevent the meat becoming tough and help it absorb all the flavours. Simmer the chicken in the poaching liquor for about 15 minutes, turning once, then transfer the cooked breasts or legs to a plate and set aside to rest. Keep a few tablespoons of the poaching liquor back for dressing the chicken.

Meanwhile, cook the rice according to the instructions on the packet so it's ready when the chicken has rested. Add the hojicha to the pan so it cooks with and infuses the rice.

Combine the reserved poaching liquor with the rice wine, rice vinegar, sesame oil, soy sauce and remaining brown sugar. Warm the dressing gently to dissolve the sugar, then allow to cool before pouring into a small jug.

Once rested, slice the chicken and plate up over the rice with the salad and greens on the side. Drizzle the dressing over the chicken, then generously scatter with the toasted sesame seeds and sliced spring onions.

DESSERTS

Earl Grey, green tea, sticky chai and white tea all feature in this mouth-watering chapter of sweet recipes. Whether you're looking for an indulgent pud to round off your Sunday roast, an afternoon pick-me-up or iced summer refreshment, these treats have got you covered.

BLACK TEA BAKED BREAKFAST DOUGHNUTS

Preparation time: 40-50 minutes, plus overnight chilling // Cooking time: 40 minutes // Makes 12 doughnuts

This recipe has been a favourite of ours for quite a few years now. It's banana bread meets cake, not too sweet and perfect for a relaxing weekend brunch. We've made it gluten-free and vegan but you could use wheat flour and dairy milk with equally delicious results.

250ml soya milk

2 heaped tsp loose leaf black tea (we love Batch Breakfast)

120g banana, peeled and broken into chunks (1 medium-sized ripe banana)

300g gluten-free self-raising flour (we love Doves Farm)

½ tsp xanthan gum (omit this if using wheat flour)

1 ½ tsp bicarbonate of soda

230g granulated sugar (you can use coconut sugar or 50:50 white and brown sugar if preferred)

250ml sunflower oil

A day in advance, warm the milk and tea gently on a low heat until starting to infuse, which should take about 5 minutes. Cool, decant, cover and place in the fridge overnight. You can infuse the milk without heating it but the flavour will develop more slowly so allow extra time.

The next day, preheat the oven to 160°c. Place the banana in a mixing bowl and beat to a smooth paste. For best results, use an electric mixer, but you can do this by hand. Sift the flour, xanthan gum and bicarbonate of soda into the bowl, then add the sugar and pour in the oil. Beat again to form a smooth dough. If using a stand mixer, this will take 1-2 minutes. The mixture is ready when the dough starts to soften again and sticks to the sides of the bowl.

Strain the soya milk into a jug, discarding the tea. Add the milk to the dough a third at a time, mixing and scraping down the bowl between each addition. You should end up with a smooth, quite runny batter.

Place two 6-hole silicone doughnut moulds on a baking sheet and spoon the mixture into the moulds. Bake in the preheated oven for 40 minutes.

Once cooked, remove from the oven and set aside for a few minutes. When cool enough to handle, remove the doughnuts by giving each cavity a little stretch to loosen, then tipping each mould upside down onto a cooling rack. The doughnuts are now the right way up!

To serve

Once fully cool, fill the centre of the doughnuts with fresh berries, dust with icing sugar, and enjoy with a scoop of coconut yoghurt and a pot of tea.

Tips

The doughnuts can be eaten right away or stored in an airtight container for 3-4 days. Our top tip is to freeze them all, then defrost one at a time as you require them. If preferred, you can make muffins instead with this recipe, which will make approximately 14. Fill each muffin case to about two thirds and bake for approximately 25 minutes until golden.

YAY! FLAPJACKS

Marc met Beth from Yay! Flapjacks on a radio show many moons ago and fell in love with their vegan and gluten-free sweet treats: incredible flapjacks and doughnuts made to their secret recipe and just oh so beautiful to look at. Talk about Instagrammable food! They deliver nationwide too. Find Yay! Flapjacks at www.yayflapjacks.co.uk or @yayflapjacks on social media.

EARL GREY MISO MALVA PUDDING

Preparation time: 20-30 minutes // Cooking time: 35 minutes // Makes 12

An indulgent dessert with South African origins from a wonderful restaurant in Sheffield. Easy to make but simply stunning. Head chef Matt created this dish especially for a collaboration dining and cocktails event that we co-hosted, and it went down an absolute storm. It's sure to impress your guests!

280g plain flour

3 tsp baking powder

1 ¼ tsp bicarbonate of soda

400g caster sugar

4 large eggs

3 tbsp dark miso

2 tbsp loose leaf Earl Grey tea (or 3 teabags)

160g apricot jam

4 tbsp (60g) butter, melted

1 tsp apple cider vinegar

500ml whole milk

For the sauce

100ml double cream

80g caster sugar

60g butter

2 tbsp water

Line a 35 by 24cm brownie tin with baking paper and preheat the oven to 180°c. In a mixing bowl, combine the flour, baking powder and bicarbonate of soda. With an electric whisk and a separate bowl, or in a stand mixer, beat the sugar, eggs, miso and tea (tear the teabags if using to add just the leaves inside) until the mixture has tripled in volume and you have a thick, pourable batter.

Beat the apricot jam into the batter, followed by the melted butter and vinegar. Continue whisking while you alternate between adding a third of the milk, then a third of the flour mix, until everything has been added and combined. Pour the mixture into your prepared tin and bake for 35 minutes.

While the pudding is in the oven, make the sauce. Gently heat the cream, sugar, butter and water in a saucepan, whisking until the butter has melted and the sugar has dissolved.

Remove the pudding from the oven, prick the surface with a fork and pour over the sauce. Leave it to rest in the tin for 10 to 15 minutes, before portioning and serving with custard.

Tips

You don't have to eat the whole pudding all at once! If you've left it to cool and want it warming up nicely, you can reheat a single portion in a 200°c oven for around 3 minutes.

THE ORANGE BIRD

We think that The Orange Bird has to be Sheffield's best new restaurant, in the heart of Hillsborough, the city's most up and coming area. Fine dining South African themed plates finished on the braai and just packed full of flavour in an intimate setting. Find them at www.theorangebird.co.uk or @theorangebirdkitchen on Instagram.

EARL GREY POACHED PEAR WITH COINTREAU CRÈME FRAICHE

Preparation time: 5 minutes // Cooking time: 30 minutes // Serves 4

Top off your dinner party with this little restaurant-style wonder. It's simple to make but your guests will be wowed by the combination of sweet and juicy pears with citrus and tea depth, rounded out with a delicious, fruity, boozy cream.

6g loose leaf Earl Grey tea (or 2 teabags)

500ml freshly boiled water

150g caster sugar

A few strips of orange zest

1 star anise

4 pears

125ml crème fraiche

15ml Cointreau

2 tbsp icing sugar

1 tsp vanilla essence

½ orange, zested

Steep the tea in the freshly boiled water in a pan for 3 minutes and then remove the leaves or teabags. Add the sugar, orange zest and star anise to the tea liquor. Bring to the boil then lower the heat to a simmer. Once the sugar has dissolved, slice the pears in half lengthways and place them into the syrup. Poach for around 15 minutes, or until tender.

While the pears are cooking, prepare the crème fraiche by adding the Cointreau, icing sugar, vanilla essence and orange zest. Stir well to combine everything.

Once tender, remove the pears from the poaching liquor with a slotted spoon and serve in bowls with a good helping of the syrup poured over the top. Add a dollop of the flavoured crème fraiche to each bowl and enjoy.

GREEN TEA LEMON CURD PAVLOVAS

Preparation time: 3 hours // Cooking time: 1 hour // Serves 6-8

A sunny celebration of summer flavours, combining the zing of fresh lemons and the earthiness of green tea. These simple pavlovas combine crisp and chewy meringue with the refreshing lightness of lemon curd swirled through soft whipped cream.

For the green tea lemon curd

100g butter

2 tbsp fragrant green tea (Mao Feng or Korea's Sejak work well)

200g caster or granulated sugar

3 lemons

4 large eggs

For the pavlovas

4 large egg whites

200g caster sugar

2 tsp cornflour

1 tsp white wine vinegar

Whipped cream or Greek yoghurt (to decorate)

For the green tea lemon curd

Melt the butter in a small pan over a very low heat. Once melted, add the tea leaves to the pan and allow them to steep in the liquid butter for 15 minutes. Add the sugar to a large heatproof bowl, then grate in the lemon zest and squeeze the lemon juice into the bowl.

Use a tea strainer to strain the melted butter into the lemon and sugar, removing the leaves. Place the bowl over a pan of gently simmering water and allow the ingredients to gently warm together for a minute.

Crack the eggs into a separate bowl and beat them together. Gradually pour the eggs into the butter mixture, whisking constantly. Continue whisking for 5-10 minutes until the mixture has warmed and thickened to the texture of custard. Pour your cooked lemon curd into a heatproof jug before decanting into sealable containers. Allow to cool, then refrigerate until ready to use.

For the pavlovas

Preheat your oven to 160°c/140°c fan/gas mark 3 and line two large baking trays with greaseproof or parchment paper.

In a large bowl, use a free-standing mixer or electric whisk to whip the egg whites to soft peaks. This should take 2-5 minutes. While whisking, add the sugar one spoonful at a time until you have a thick, glossy meringue mixture that holds its peaks. Whisk the cornflour and vinegar into the meringue mixture until combined.

Spoon 6-8 dollops of meringue onto your lined trays, using the back of the spoon to roughly shape them into nests. Place the trays in the preheated oven and immediately turn the heat down to 140°c/120°c fan/gas mark 1. Bake for 30 minutes, before turning the oven off and leaving them in there for a further 30 minutes to cool slightly – this ensures they won't crack when exposed to cool air. Remove the trays from the oven and allow the baked meringues to cool completely.

To serve

Once cooled, top the meringues with a little whipped cream followed by a generous blob of your cooled green tea lemon curd, and enjoy!

MAVERICK BAKING

Maverick Baking is Scotland-based Instagram baker/blogger and all-round lovely lady Kelly; a self-taught baker and chocolate addict. Kelly delivers a baking blog full of sweet recipes and tips, with loads of simple bakes that even those with kitchen-fright and no fancy kitchen equipment can whip up! Find her at www.maverickbaking.com or @maverickbaking on Instagram.

GREEN TEA MOCHI

Preparation time: 25 minutes // Serves 4-5

Mochi is probably best known as a small glutinous rice cake from Japan but is also enjoyed in South Korea and it was there, at the Puruncha Tea Institute in Daegu, then we learnt about this delicious snack. Mrs Soh is their chef in residence, and she has more recipes up her sleeve that we've had hot meals. Many of the incredible delicacies she serves up are closely guarded secrets, but we're lucky enough to get the inside scoop on this one. Traditionally, mochi is made by pounding glutinous rice into a powder which takes time and effort. However, these days we can buy the flour in an Asian supermarket and speed up the process even more with a microwave.

300g glutinous or sweet rice flour

100g icing sugar

2 tsp ground Korean green tea or matcha

½ tsp salt

300ml water

Cornflour, for dusting

Your choice of filling

Mochi are super simple to make but they can easily turn into a sticky mess if you don't take care, so prepare your cooking space and measure your ingredients carefully. For the filling, you can use anything you want really. Red bean paste is traditional and can be picked up in any Asian supermarket, but people use cookie dough, peanut butter, strawberries and even ice cream.

Sieve your dry ingredients into a microwave-safe bowl (glass is best) and add the water, stirring to make a smooth paste. Microwave the mixture on full power for around 3 minutes and then stir again. Microwave for another minute and you should have a sticky but pliable dough which can be easily pulled away from the sides of the bowl.

Use cornflour to dust your hands and the work surface. After the dough has cooled slightly, form it into small balls around the size of a table tennis ball. Roll out until they're about 5cm in diameter and then put a teaspoon of your chosen filling in the middle. Pinch together the sides and coat with icing sugar or more matcha if you'd like an extra hit of tea. Place the mochi seam side down on a plate and enjoy within 24 hours.

CHOC TEA CHOC ICE

Preparation time: 30 minutes, plus 30-40 minutes cooling and 2 hours freezing // Makes 8 x 100ml choc ices

A fun recipe for kids and grown-ups to make together and enjoy on a hot day in the sunshine. Either use a choc chip tea blend or make your own from a malty Assam black tea and cocoa husks in a 1:1 ratio. The syrup and coconut milk adds just the right level of sweetness for the kids.

10g Choc Chip tea

225ml freshly boiled water

2 tbsp maple syrup (or Assam tea syrup – see page 144)

100g chocolate for melting

550ml oat milk or coconut milk

Optional Extras

2g loose leaf peppermint tea

100ml Baileys Irish Cream

Steep the tea in the freshly boiled water for 10 minutes so it's nice and strong. Strain the tea and stir in the maple or tea syrup, then refrigerate until cold.

While your tea is cooling, melt your chocolate in a bowl over a pan of boiling water. To create the crisp outer layer of the choc ice, pour the melted chocolate into a lollipop mould and rotate to make sure the inside is fully coated, then turn upside down to let the excess chocolate drain out back into the bowl. Repeat and then pop the moulds into the freezer to firm up while you prep the ice cream.

Once the sweetened tea has chilled, add the oat milk or coconut milk and stir well. Take your moulds out of the freezer and fill each one with your tea-flavoured ice cream mix, then return to the freezer to set. Wait until your choc ices are completely frozen before serving… if you can wait that long!

Tips

Add peppermint to the hot tea infusion for a mega minty choc ice! If it's a grown-ups only affair, make them super-indulgent with Baileys Irish Cream added to the oat or coconut milk.

STICKY CHAI ICE CREAM

Preparation time: 1 hour, plus chilling and freezing time // Cooking time: 30 minutes // Makes approximately 950ml

Spicy, sweet, milky chai in ice cream form? Heaven! And easy to make too. We worked with ice cream pro Yee Kwan to bring you this delicious recipe which uses a classic custard base infused with masala chai, adding all those yummy spices and malty tea depth to this luxurious ice cream.

450ml double cream

225ml milk

4 tbsp Kama Sutra Sticky Chai (or 3 tbsp dry masala chai + 1 tbsp honey)

6 egg yolks

150g white sugar

Pinch of salt

In a medium saucepan, bring the cream and milk to the boil. Stir in the sticky chai and remove the pan from the heat before allowing the mixture to steep for 45 minutes to 1 hour.

Pour the infused cream mixture through a strainer into a bowl, pressing on the tea leaves with a spoon to extract all the liquid and flavour.

In a clean saucepan, whisk the egg yolks and sugar together until pale in colour and slightly thickened. Slowly add the strained masala chai cream, whisking constantly.

Place the pan on a medium heat, stirring frequently, until a thick custard forms on the back of a spoon. Stir in a pinch of salt to taste, then strain the custard into an airtight container and chill in the fridge overnight.

The next day, churn the ice cream according to the manufacturer's instructions on your ice cream maker. Transfer to an airtight container and put in the freezer for at least 4 hours before serving.

Alternatively, if you don't have an ice cream maker, place the mixture into the freezer and take out to 'churn' using a spoon every 30 minutes for 4-6 hours until the right consistency is achieved.

Tips

To make this ice cream dairy-free, replace the milk with almond milk and the cream with coconut cream.

WHITE TEA, RASPBERRY & PROSECCO SORBET

Preparation time: 30 minutes, plus chilling and freezing time // Cooking time: 5 minutes // Serves: 6-8

A refreshing palate cleanser with an alcoholic tea twist; what's not to love? Pai Mu Dan white tea works a treat in this recipe.

200ml brewed white tea

100g caster sugar

150g raspberries

½ lemon, zested

450ml Prosecco

Discard the leaves from the brewed tea and stir the sugar into the hot liquid until dissolved. In a small saucepan, bring the sweet tea to the boil and then take it off the heat to cool. This is a white tea simple syrup. Pour into a container and refrigerate.

Meanwhile, blend the raspberries and then push the mixture through a sieve. Stir the lemon zest into the raspberry purée, then pour in around 200ml of the chilled tea syrup along with the Prosecco. Stir to combine and check the flavour; you'll need to judge the mixture by taste to see how much extra syrup to use as it will depend on the tartness of the raspberries.

Mix the sorbet in an ice cream maker according to the manufacturer's instructions. Alternatively, transfer your sorbet mixture to a shallow dish and put it straight into the freezer. Take out to stir and break up every 30 minutes or so for around 4 hours or until frozen. Continue to freeze for another 8 hours or overnight. When the sorbet is ready, garnish the scoops with sprigs of fresh mint to serve.

Tips
Don't like raspberries? Try 300ml of tangerine juice instead.

DA HONG PAO
OAT COOKIE SANDWICHES

Preparation time: 40-50 minutes // Cooking time: 25 minutes // Makes 12 cookie sandwiches (24 individual cookies)

This started as a recipe from our schooldays. It became a favourite and we adapted it into all sorts of different forms. Now we've given these oat cookies a new lease of life again, turning them into gluten-free and vegan cookie sandwiches with roasted tea and chocolate for a decadently fun treat.

For the cookies

220g butter or vegan alternative (choose one with a low water content, we love Flora Plant B+tter)

2 heaped tsp Da Hong Pao roasted loose leaf tea

220g gluten-free self-raising flour (we love Doves Farm)

180g gluten-free rolled oats

90g granulated sugar

1 ½ tsp baking powder

1 ½ tsp xanthan gum

3 tbsp golden syrup

For the buttercream filling

250g butter or vegan substitute (as above), beaten until soft

300g icing sugar

25g cocoa powder

For the tea icing

1 heaped tsp Da Hong Pao roasted loose leaf tea

100ml boiling water

300g icing sugar

Milk chocolate, finely chopped (we love Moo Free)

For the cookies

Preheat the oven to 140°c. Gently heat the butter and tea in a saucepan until melted. Remove from the heat and infuse for 5 minutes. Mix the dry ingredients together in a bowl, pour in the infused butter through a sieve, add the syrup and stir until everything is fully combined. Roll the cookie dough into 30g balls and place on two lined baking sheets. Flatten into thin circles, approximately 7-8cm in diameter. Bake the cookies for 25 minutes in the preheated oven until golden. Allow them to cool and firm up before handling. Match your cookies up into similarly-sized pairs for neater sandwiches.

For the buttercream filling

Add the icing sugar and cocoa to the softened butter, then continue to beat until light and fluffy. Take one half of each cookie pair and cover the flat side with a layer of buttercream the same thickness as the cookie. Pipe with a 5mm nozzle for best results, but you can also spread it on with a knife. Starting from the outside, pipe a circle around the edge and then spiral into the centre. Place the other cookie on top, then pop in the fridge to set.

For the tea icing

To make a concentrated Da Hong Pao tea, spoon the leaves into a heatproof bowl or mug and pour over the boiling water. Allow the tea to infuse and then cool to room temperature. Strain the tea and add the liquid to the icing sugar a spoonful at a time, mixing between additions. The perfect consistency is an icing that takes 10 seconds to return to a flat surface after stirring. Add more icing sugar if it's too runny.

Spoon some tea icing over the top of each cookie sandwich to create a puddle. Spread if necessary. Sprinkle with a little chopped chocolate and allow to set.

To serve

Enjoy with a cup of Da Hong Pao tea to bring out those chocolate notes.

YAY! FLAPJACKS

Marc met Beth from Yay! Flapjacks on a radio show many moons ago and fell in love with their vegan and gluten free sweet treats. Incredible flapjacks and doughnuts made to their secret recipe and just oh so beautiful to look at. Talk about Instagrammable food! They deliver nationwide too. Find Yay! Flapjacks at www.yayflapjacks.co.uk or @yayflapjacks on social media.

STICKY CHAI, CHOCOLATE & SESAME DOUGHNUTS

Preparation time: 45 minutes, plus 1.5 – 2.5 hours resting // Cooking time: 30-35 minutes // Makes 12 doughnuts

Batch Tea's Kama Sutra Sticky Chai packs a serious punch, which is why I couldn't resist using it for this doughnut. The deeply spiced fragrance (cardamom, cloves, cinnamon and fennel) is perfect for infusing the sweet honey crème. All finished with rich chocolate ganache and toasted sesame seeds. Enjoy!

For the dough

180g milk at room temperature

1 medium egg

20g fresh yeast (or 10g dry)

375g strong white bread flour

45g golden caster sugar

5g salt

35g soft butter

For the chai crème

50g caster sugar

25g plain flour

3 medium egg yolks

250g whole milk

10g Kama Sutra Sticky Chai

150g whipping cream

1 tbsp (20g) runny honey

To cook

Vegetable oil

To finish

75g whipping cream

75g dark and milk chocolate (use half of each)

20g sesame seeds, toasted until golden

For the dough

Whisk the milk, egg and yeast together in a large bowl until the yeast has softened, then add the flour, sugar and salt. Mix with a dough scraper until everything starts to come together into a rough dough. Dimple in the butter with your fingertips, then turn the dough out onto a clean table and knead without any additional flour for 10 minutes. Shape into a ball and place it back into the bowl. Sprinkle with flour, cover with an upturned bowl and rest at room temperature for 90-120 minutes. Meanwhile, make the chai crème.

For the chai crème

Whisk half the sugar with the flour and egg yolks. Bring the milk and remaining sugar just up to the boil and then remove from the heat, add the chai tea and leave to infuse for 4 minutes. Strain the milk into the egg mixture and whisk together, then pour the milk mixture back into the pan and set over a medium heat. Bring to the boil, stirring all the time, and cook for 2 minutes. Pour the chai custard into a bowl, cover the surface with clingfilm and cool before refrigerating. Whip the cream to soft peaks, then fold in the honey. Beat the chilled chai custard to soften, then add the honey whipped cream and fold together gently until soft and silky. Refrigerate until needed.

To shape and cook the doughnuts

Flatten the rested dough on a lightly dusted surface, then divide into 12 pieces around 55g each. Roll into tight balls, then use a rolling pin to flatten each one very slightly. Place on two lightly oiled trays, brush the tops lightly with a little more oil and cover loosely with cling film. Rest for 60-90 minutes. Heat the vegetable oil in a deep fryer or pan to 180°c. Lower the doughnuts into the fryer, 3 or 4 at a time, and cook for 30 seconds, then turn over to cook the other side for 30 seconds so the outside is sealed. Continue frying for a further 2 minutes on each side. Drain and cool on kitchen paper.

To finish

Heat the cream to just below boiling point and pour it over the chocolate. Let it sit for a minute or so before stirring into a glossy ganache. Slice your doughnuts open like a sandwich. Spoon around 35-40g of your chai crème onto each doughnut base. Upturn the lids and dunk the tops in the chocolate ganache, then place on the crème. Sprinkle with toasted sesame seeds and leave to set before eating if you can help it!

BAKE WITH JACK

Jack Sturgess, aka Bake With Jack, is a professional chef turned bread maker and educator on a mission to give you the knowledge you need to make amazing bread at home for life. He demystifies the breadmaking process while using his experience as a chef to create something delicious to go with it. He's also Channel 4's Sunday Brunch Bread Expert and all-round ridiculously nice guy. Go check him out at bakewithjack.co.uk or social media channels @bakewithjack. You'll love him as much as we do!

BAKING

Tea has a long history of being used in baking, from the matcha sponge cake of Japan to the barmbrack of Ireland. Whether you're using powdered tea in batters or soaking ingredients such as dried fruit in a hot brew, there's a whole world of flavours to discover that will take your breads, cakes and biscuits up a level. Just remember to think outside the box and experiment!

FRUIT TEA BREAD

Preparation time: 30 minutes, plus overnight soaking // Cooking time: 1 hour 30 minutes // Serves 10-12

This is a loaf of many names: in Wales, it's known as bara brith. In Ireland it's brack. It's also known as speckled, freckled or mottled bread. Whatever you decide to call it, the loaf itself is dense, moist and full of flavour. The ingredients for this tea bread vary from region to region. Some include yeast and produce a fruited bread whereas this recipe uses baking powder or self-raising flour and is closer to a cake. I was first introduced to it by my now 101-year-old grandmother. This is her recipe, though I've added some spices to give it a bit of extra zing.

150g currants

150g sultanas

150g brown sugar

2 oranges, zested

300ml strong black tea

275g self-raising flour

1 egg, beaten

2-3 tsp mixed spice or 2 tsp cinnamon, 1 tsp ground ginger and a pinch of nutmeg (optional)

Put the dried fruit, sugar and orange zest in a large bowl. Pour over the hot tea, give it a good stir and then leave it to stand overnight.

The next day, grease and line a loaf tin or 20cm round cake tin. Stir the flour, beaten egg and spices (if using) into the steeped fruit and mix thoroughly.

Transfer the mixture into the tin and bake in a preheated oven at 150°c for 1 hour 30 minutes. Leave to cool on a wire rack before slicing and serving.

Tips

This freezes really well. Defrost at room temperature for 4 to 5 hours.

MOONBEAM SHORTBREAD

Preparation time: 1 hour 10 minutes // Cooking time: 45 minutes // Serves 8

What started off as a trial run for tea-infused biscuits became a firm favourite in our Tea House. This buttery shortbread is a real treat thanks to the contrast of sharp citrus and floral lavender with the subtle bite of Ceylon black tea. The perfect accompaniment to your afternoon cuppa!

125g butter, at room temperature

50g caster sugar, plus extra to finish

2 tsp Arthur Dove Tea Co Moonbeam loose leaf tea

150g plain flour

50g cornflour

Pinch of salt

Splash of milk

Use a wooden spoon and large bowl or a free-standing mixer to cream the butter with the caster sugar until pale and smooth. Use a rubber spatula to scrape down the sides and mix everything in, leaving zero waste!

Use a pestle and mortar to grind the tea leaves into a fine dust. You don't want any big crunchy bits as it can be a bit hard on the teeth. Add a splash of hot water to the ground leaves and throw them into the butter and sugar mixture. Stir to combine.

Sift the flour, cornflour and salt into the bowl and mix it all together. If the dough seems a little too dry, add a splash of milk.

Lightly dust a sheet of greaseproof paper with a little plain flour and press or roll the dough out into an approximately 20cm disc. Carefully lift the dough with the greaseproof paper onto a baking tray. Gently mark out eight sections with a knife and pinch the edges to crimp them decoratively. Use a fork to prick the dough and chill for 30 minutes to an hour.

When the dough is nearly chilled, preheat the oven to 150°c. Bake the shortbread in the middle of the oven for 45 minutes to 1 hour until lightly golden. Remove from the oven and sprinkle with a little more caster sugar if you like.

Cool the shortbread on the baking tray for 10 minutes and then slide onto a wire rack to cool completely before cutting and serving with your favourite pot of tea, or perhaps a pot of Moonbeam?

BISCUIT & BREW TEA HOUSE

This family-run tea house in the heart of Nottingham serves a range of loose leaf teas alongside delicious food, sweet treats and tea-based cookery goodness. Run by Dee and her partner Darren, of the awesome Arthur Dove Tea Company. Find them at 12 Hounds Gate, Nottingham, NG1 7AB, arthurdoveteaco.com or @biscuitandbrewteahouse on social media.

BANANA BREAD TEA LOAF

Preparation time: 10 minutes // Cooking time: 50-60 minutes // Serves 10

Created on a rainy day, this is a sweet and cake-like banana bread infused with Arthur Dove Tea Co's Banana Fudge black tea. Whip it up in minutes and serve warm or cold! A slice (or two) pairs perfectly with your beverage of choice… if it isn't Banana Fudge, you've gone bananas.

300g banana and avocado (peeled weight)

125g butter, melted

125g caster sugar

3 heaped tsp Arthur Dove Tea Co Banana Fudge loose leaf tea

25ml hot water

1 tsp vanilla extract

½ tsp cinnamon

2 eggs

175g plain flour

1 ½ tsp baking powder

½ tsp bicarbonate of soda

50g walnuts, chopped

Preheat the oven to 160°c. Grease a one pound loaf tin and line it with a loaf tin liner or greaseproof paper.

Mash the banana and avocado in a bowl, then stir in the melted butter and sugar.

Meanwhile, infuse the Banana Fudge tea in the hot water. You can use any black tea here or skip this step, but Banana Fudge is, in our opinion, the best to use in this recipe. Let it steep for about 3 minutes to make a liquid concentrate, then strain or remove the tea infuser.

Stir the vanilla, cinnamon and tea-infused liquid into the banana mixture. Beat in the eggs, then sift the flour, baking powder and bicarb into the bowl and mix well. Fold in the chopped nuts, leaving a few for decoration. Pour the cake mixture evenly into the loaf tin and top with the reserved nuts.

Bake in the preheated oven for 50 minutes to 1 hour, testing the centre with a thin skewer. When the skewer comes out clean, the banana bread is done. Let it rest in the tin for 10 minutes and then lift out with the greaseproof paper or liner to cool on a wire rack.

Once cooled, slice up the banana bread to your liking and enjoy warm or cold with butter, or even a cheeky drizzle of maple syrup!

BISCUIT & BREW TEA HOUSE

This family-run tea house in the heart of Nottingham serves a range of loose leaf teas alongside delicious food, sweet treats and tea-based cookery goodness. Run by Dee and her partner Darren, of the awesome Arthur Dove Tea Company. Find them at 12 Hounds Gate, Nottingham, NG1 7AB, arthurdoveteaco.com or @biscuitandbrewteahouse on social media.

Moonbeam Shortbread

Fruit Tea Bread

Banana Bread
Tea Loaf

MATCHA MUSHI-PAN (JAPANESE STEAMED SPONGE CAKE)

Preparation time: 15 minutes // Cooking time: 10 minutes // Makes 12 cakes

◇◇

This recipe uses matcha to add flavour to a traditional light and airy Japanese steamed sponge cake.

◇◇

130g plain flour

12g matcha

10g baking powder

2 eggs

120ml milk

50g caster sugar

50ml canola oil

Prepare a large steamer (if you don't have a steamer these buns can be baked) with 3-4cm of cold water in the base. Line 12 ramekins or small heatproof dishes with cupcake cases. You can also use silicone moulds.

In a bowl, combine the flour, matcha and baking powder until well mixed. In another bowl, whisk the eggs, milk, sugar and oil together. Slowly add the wet mixture to the flour mixture and fold together until smooth.

Spoon the batter evenly into the prepared cases and steam over a high heat for around 8 minutes. They are ready when a skewer inserted into the centre comes out clean.

Leave to cool for 10-15 minutes. These are best served slightly warm.

SAVOURY TEA BREAD

Preparation time: 30 minutes, plus 2 hours proving // Cooking time: 25-30 minutes // Makes 1 loaf

This nice twist on a classic herby loaf uses malty Chinese black tea. Great with butter and cheese! Replace the black tea with your preferred tea to mix it up.

15g whole leaf Chinese black tea

1 litre boiling water

500g white bread flour

1 x 7g sachet of instant yeast

1 tbsp sugar

1 tsp salt

2 tbsp olive oil

Steep the tea in the boiling water for 3 minutes and then remove the leaves but don't discard them. Keep around 400ml of the tea liquor for the bread and allow it to cool until lukewarm. You can drink the rest! If the leaves are still firm or wiry you can steep them again until they're a little softer.

Reserving just a few of the whole leaves for decoration later, blitz the softened tea leaves with about 100ml of the tea liquor in a blender until smooth.

Put all the remaining ingredients plus the blitzed tea leaves and 250ml of the tea liquor into the bowl of a stand mixer. Mix for 10 minutes on medium speed with a dough hook attachment. If you don't have a stand mixer, combine the dry ingredients first and then slowly add the wet ingredients while stirring until the dough comes together, then knead it for 10 minutes.

Once you have a smooth dough, shape it into a ball and place in a greased bowl. Cover with cling film and leave to rise for 1 hour or until doubled in size.

Line a baking tray with baking paper and knock back the dough by punching the air out of it and pulling the edges of the dough inwards, then reshape into a ball and place on the baking paper to prove for a further hour, again until doubled in size.

Preheat the oven to 220°c/200°c fan/gas mark 7. Dust the proved loaf with a little flour and cut a cross in the top with a sharp knife. Gently rehydrate the reserved tea leaves and place them on top of the loaf for decoration, pulling out the edges of the leaves to give them a nice shape. They'll crisp up nicely as the bread bakes.

Bake the bread in the preheated oven for 25-30 minutes until the loaf sounds hollow when tapped underneath or the internal temperature of the bread is 93°c. Transfer the bread to a wire rack and let it cool for at least an hour before tucking in.

STORE CUPBOARD & SIDES

Here we're showcasing the versatility of tea with a host of sweet and savoury ways to season your food with fantastic flavours. Lots of these store cupboard favourites – such as jams, chutneys, salt and syrup – will last for a long time when properly stored, so are great options for a spot of batch cooking (pun intended). Others make great snacks or accompaniments to main meals, but all of them offer something a little bit different that we hope you'll keep coming back for.

SMOKY HOUMOUS TWO WAYS

Preparation time: 10 minutes (for each version) // Cooking time: 45 minutes (Version 2 only) // Serves 4

Lapsang souchong is such a versatile ingredient and adds a delicious smokiness to healthy homemade houmous for a real treat. We've given you two versions of the recipe here: Marc's doesn't involve any cooking and Owen's starts by infusing dried chickpeas with lapsang souchong. Try them both and pick your favourite!

Version 1 (Marc)

1 x 400g tin of chickpeas

½ tsp ground cumin or cumin seeds

4g loose leaf Lapsang Souchong tea

3 tbsp extra virgin olive oil

1 clove of garlic, peeled

1 tbsp tahini

½ tsp salt

½ lemon, juiced

Version 2 (Owen)

10g plus 1 tsp (approx. 2g) loose leaf Lapsang Souchong tea

100g dried chickpeas

½ tsp bicarbonate of soda

Pinch of salt

50g tahini

1 lemon, juiced

1 clove of garlic, crushed

2 tbsp extra virgin olive oil

Version 1 (Marc)

Drain and thoroughly rinse the tinned chickpeas. Put the cumin and tea leaves into a food processor and whizz until quite fine (but far from being dust!) as the coarser the leaves, the more texture they'll add to the hummus but large pieces will be too hard and bitter.

Add the chickpeas, olive oil, garlic, tahini, salt and lemon juice to the processor. Whizz until the houmous is smooth enough for your liking, then taste and add more lemon juice or salt as desired. Decant the houmous into a serving bowl, then garnish with a drizzle of extra virgin olive oil, a few cumin seeds, pumpkin seeds and fresh coriander leaves. This super simple Mediterranean dip is great served as part of a mezze or with crudités, salad and warm pittas for a light meal.

Version 2 (Owen)

Bring a litre of water to the boil in a large pan. Place the 10g of tea leaves in a muslin cloth or single-use teabag, tie the top and drop into the pan. Alternatively, use 2 lapsang souchong teabags. Add the dried chickpeas, bicarbonate of soda and salt. Cook until the chickpeas are soft, then drain and transfer to a blender.

Grind the teaspoon of loose leaf tea into a fine powder in a spice mill or using a pestle and mortar. Add this to the blender along with the tahini, lemon juice, crushed garlic and olive oil. Blend until everything is combined to a smooth consistency, then transfer to a serving dish and enjoy.

Tips

Powdered lapsang souchong is great whenever you want to add a hint of smokiness to a recipe. Use it as a rub for meat or combine with mince for burgers. You can also add a few teaspoons to soups and stews, or other dips like baba ghanoush.

GREEN TEA SALAD DRESSING

Preparation time: 5 minutes // Makes 1 portion

◇◇◇

Did you know that you can eat tea leaves? They're basically a herb and can be used as such: dried and added to your cooking, powdered and used like a spice, or rehydrated (fresh is even better if you can get the leaves straight from the bush!) and added to eggs, sauces or dressings like this one.

◇◇◇

20g loose leaf green tea (something like Dragonwell or Sencha works well)

300ml water at 80°c

1 clove of garlic

½ tsp salt

1 tbsp white vinegar

3 tbsp good quality salad oil (I like using a garlic or oak smoked rapeseed oil myself)

First steep and then strain the tea. This rehydrates the leaves and you get a tasty brew to drink while making the dressing.

Let the leaves cool to room temperature while you peel and chop the garlic. Blitz the tea leaves, garlic and salt in a food processor. You don't want a fine paste, so just pulse to combine. Add the vinegar and oil for the final pulse, then taste and adjust as needed.

Use as a dressing on your favourite leafy salad. Amazing!

GREEN TEA SAUCE

Preparation time: 5 minutes // Cooking time: 15 minutes // Serves 4

◇◇◇

Another way to incorporate tea into your supper is to use green tea leaves in a traditional parsley sauce instead of the herb. Great with fish and eggs.

◇◇◇

25g butter

20g plain flour

1 tsp English mustard (optional)

250ml milk, plus extra if needed

Handful of loose leaf green tea

Freshly ground pepper, to taste

Sea salt, to taste

In a medium-sized saucepan, melt the butter over a medium heat. Stir in the flour and mustard (if using) to form a thick paste. Cook gently for 2 to 3 minutes, watching the heat to ensure the paste does not burn.

Gradually whisk in the milk and bring to the boil. Add the tea leaves and simmer for 5 minutes, stirring frequently to make sure there are no lumps. The sauce should be quite thick but still pouring consistency. If it becomes too thick, add a little more milk.

Season with a few grinds of black pepper and a good pinch of sea salt. Taste and add more as needed, then serve and enjoy.

EARL GREY CARROTS

Preparation time: 5 minutes // Cooking time: 10-15 minutes // Serves 4 as a side

This idea came from a chef making Ceylon tea-inspired delicacies in Sri Lanka, but it's certainly not localised to that region. If you're looking to add a flavourful twist to your meals, infusing your boiled or steamed vegetables with tea is an easy and delicious trick. For this recipe we're using carrots but have a play around and see what works. Smoky lapsang parsnips anyone?

10g loose leaf Earl Grey tea
8 carrots

As straightforward as it sounds. The Earl Grey adds delicate citrus notes to the carrots and makes this an even healthier side dish. First, put the tea leaves into a muslin cloth or single-use teabag and tie the top. Alternatively, use 5 Earl Grey teabags. Cut the carrots however you prefer, fill a saucepan with water and bring to the boil.

Boil the carrots and tea in the pan of water until the veg is cooked to your liking (I prefer mine al dente). If you like roasted carrots, try par boiling them this way and then coating in a little maple syrup and dusting with ground Earl Grey tea leaves before roasting.

TEA INFUSED BULGUR WHEAT

Preparation time: 5 minutes // Cooking time: 15-20 minutes // Serves 4 as a side

Bulgur wheat makes a delicious side dish for autumnal savoury recipes, and works beautifully as the base for a healthy salad or buddha bowl. Add black tea for a little extra depth and malty savouriness. Any tea works really but we like a higher grade Assam tea for added fruitiness and maltiness.

5g loose leaf Assam FTGFOP grade black tea
500ml freshly boiled water
160g bulgur wheat
Salt and pepper, to taste

Steep the tea leaves in the freshly boiled water for 4 minutes, then strain the liquid into the pan. Add the bulgur wheat, salt and pepper to the pan and bring to the boil. Cook for 10-15 minutes until the water has been absorbed and the bulgur wheat is tender with just enough bite. If the water dries out too quickly, just add a little more. When ready, fluff with a fork and serve.

Tips
You can also prepare the bulgur wheat by covering it with the hot tea liquor to soak for about 25 minutes, again until the water has been absorbed. Soaking will result in a little more bite and chewiness which is lovely where the bulgur wheat is the star of the show, such as in a salad or bowl.

TEA SALT

Preparation time: 5 minutes // Makes 200g

This is a fantastic seasoning to have on hand for a variety of recipes. Use different teas to create different effects in your meals with a good quality coarse sea salt or rock salt. We like to use Himalayan pink salt with a Dan Cong oolong tea or Maldon sea salt with a malty black tea.

100g loose leaf tea

100g coarse sea or rock salt

If you're using whole tea leaves, you'll want to break them up, but you don't want a powder, so use a pestle and mortar or even just a small bowl inside a big bowl to break your loose tea leaves into smaller pieces. If you're using a broken leaf tea you might get away with skipping this step.

Combine the broken tea and the salt in a big bowl and mix well. Decant the mix into your salt grinder. Any leftovers can be stored in an airtight container for over a year.

MATCHA CHILLI PEANUTS

Preparation time: 10 minutes, plus dehydrating // Cooking time: 15-20 minutes // Makes approx. 300g

When Owen lived in Sydney, Australia, he experimented with different ways to use tea. He partnered with a small, independent chilli sauce company called The Chilli Effect to develop matcha and chilli flavoured peanuts. This recipe is super simple and perfect for a quick snack or when you need nibbles for an event.

40g pickled jalapeños (drained weight) or 2 tbsp chilli powder

10g matcha

250g raw shelled peanuts

2 tbsp olive oil

First, you'll need to dehydrate the jalapeños if using. Dry the drained chilli peppers using kitchen towel to speed up the process and then either use a dehydrator or put them on a sheet of greaseproof paper in the oven at its lowest temperature for a few hours until the chillies are completely dry and crisp.

Grind the dried jalapeños to a fine powder in a spice grinder or pestle and mortar and mix with the matcha. If not using jalapeños, simply combine the chilli powder and matcha. Toss the peanuts in the olive oil and then add the chilli matcha powder. Toss until evenly coated and then spread out on a sheet of baking paper and bake at 180°c for 15-20 minutes.

Leave to cool completely before eating and store in an airtight container for up to 3 months.

Matcha Chilli Peanuts

Tomato & Date
Tea Chutney

Lapsang Souchong
Plum Jam

Green Tea
Salad Dressing

Smoky Houmous

Tea Salt

LAPSANG SOUCHONG PLUM JAM

Preparation time: 20 minutes // Cooking time: 1 hour, plus setting/chilling time // Makes 1.5kg

Having a cup of tea with a slice of jammy toast is always a delicious snack. So how about doubling up on the tea and loading up your spread with a handful of the good stuff too? This recipe would work with all sorts of fruits and teas so play around with the flavours and see what you come up with!

20g loose leaf Lapsang Souchong tea

150ml water

1kg plums

1kg jam sugar

1 lemon, juiced

1 cinnamon stick (optional)

2 whole star anise (optional)

Jam is pretty straightforward really, you throw everything in a pan and get it cooking. The key is to get the sugar or pectin content and the temperature right, so that the jam sets properly. Different fruits have different amounts of pectin, just to keep things interesting, so enjoy experimenting to come up with your favourite combinations.

For this one, we're using a nice Lapsang Souchong tea to impart a sweet, smoky flavour in the plums. Other combinations which work well are strawberry or blackberry with Earl Grey, green tea and raspberry or even a spicy masala chai marmalade.

There are a couple of ways to do this. You can either steep the tea in the water and use that as your liquid component when making the jam, or alternatively you can make a big teabag using a jam cloth or muslin and throw it in with the fruit and water for the full boil. For this recipe we're using the latter method.

Use a square of muslin or a jam cloth to hold your tea leaves and tie securely at the top. Add this to a large heavy-based pan containing the water and destoned plums. If you're using one or both of the whole spices, add these in here too. Bring the liquid to the boil and simmer for 45-50 minutes, stirring occasionally until the plums are soft and the liquid has reduced.

Slowly add the sugar, stirring until it all dissolves, then add the lemon juice and bring it back to a rolling boil for 5-7 minutes to reach the setting point. If you have a jam thermometer, this is 105°c. Otherwise you can test this by putting a plate in the freezer and when you've finished the boil take the plate out and put a drop of jam on the frozen plate. If the jam sets, job done. If not, keep boiling the mixture for another minute or two. When the jam is ready, discard the tea and whole spices (if used) before pouring the hot jam into sterilised jars and sealing with the lids.

TOMATO & DATE TEA CHUTNEY

Preparation time: 1 hour, plus soaking overnight // Cooking time: 1 hour // Makes 8 x 290g jars

To avoid the tea flavours being overwhelmed, this chutney doesn't use spicy ingredients and incorporates more subtle ones. I think the tea works well with the dates and sultanas. This recipe uses Kama Sutra Sticky Chai, but each tea will offer different flavours. Try with your favourite tea.

20g Batch Tea Kama Sutra Sticky Chai

300ml freshly boiled water

200g sultanas

500g onions

1kg fresh tomatoes

40g fresh ginger

500g Bramley apples

375g soft dates

400ml red wine vinegar

½ tbsp salt

300g soft dark brown sugar

Soak the tea in the almost boiling water for as long as possible, ideally 1 hour. Strain the tea to leave 250ml of liquid and discard the tea leaves. Soak the sultanas in the tea and leave for at least 1 hour or overnight.

Before cooking the chutney, sterilise your jars. To do this, preheat the oven to 120°c and place the clean jars on a clean baking sheet in the oven for 20 minutes. The lids can be sterilised in boiling water for 5 minutes.

Place the onions in a food processor and pulse until finely chopped. Blitz the tomatoes in the food processor separately until roughly chopped. Place the tomatoes in a sieve and leave for 15 minutes to drain off the liquid. Meanwhile, peel the ginger and apples, then dice into 0.5cm and 1cm cubes respectively. Destone and roughly chop the dates.

Put a large saucepan on a low-medium heat and cook the onions and ginger in the red wine vinegar and salt for 5 minutes, or until the onions are soft. Now add the apples and dates and cook for approximately 15 minutes, stirring regularly. Once the mixture is hot, add the sugar and stir to incorporate. Cook the chutney for approximately 45 minutes, stirring regularly.

To test whether the chutney is cooked, use the spoon to create a furrow on the surface. If the furrow isn't filled in with cooking liquor, the chutney should be ready. Turn the heat down to the lowest setting and use a ladle and funnel to fill the sterilised jars, leaving 1cm of space below the rim. Screw the lids on tightly and leave to cool. For the best flavour, keep the jars sealed for a couple of weeks before opening. Serve the chutney with any cheeses or as a burger relish.

MATTHEW HULLEY (JUST PRESERVES)

Just Preserves make delicious handmade jams, marmalades, chutneys and pickles to the highest standards using the open pan method. Ingredients are sourced locally where possible, with fruit and vegetables bought at Sheffield Wholesale Markets very early in the morning! The results are tasty products for the folk of Sheffield and beyond. Find them at justpreserves.co.uk or farmers' markets around Sheffield.

TEA EGGS

Preparation time: 20 minutes, plus 24 hours marinating // Cooking time: 5 minutes // Makes 6

We fell in love with tea eggs while travelling around China and finding them alongside baozi in any good street food area or 7-Eleven! They're beautifully maarbled, deliciously sweet and savoury and can be eaten on their own as a snack or as a delicious addition to a noodle soup.

6 organic free-range eggs (we tend to use hen eggs but feel free to go crazy!)

500ml water

60ml light soy sauce

20ml dark soy sauce

1 tbsp Shaoxing rice wine

Thumb-sized piece of fresh ginger

2 cinnamon quills

4 star anise

4 cloves

1 bay leaf

1 tbsp dried orange peel

4 tsp loose leaf shou (ripe) pu'er tea

2 tsp sugar

2 tsp sea salt

1 tsp Sichuan peppercorns

If you keep your eggs in the fridge, remove them 1 hour before preparing. Meanwhile, make the marinade by adding all the other ingredients to a medium saucepan. Boil for 10 minutes and then leave to cool before removing the tea leaves.

Hard boil your eggs for about 6 minutes in a pan of water, then run them under cold water or set aside to cool. Once the eggs are cool enough to handle, the fun begins! Gently crack the shells with the back of a spoon, hard enough to allow the marinade through but not so much it results in a 'bleed' which will just result in a brown blotch on the egg. This is how you create the marble effect.

Pop the cracked eggs gently back into the cooled marinade, making sure the eggs are fully covered in the liquid, and leave for 24 hours. You can marinate them in a sealable bag or just a small enough container to ensure the eggs are fully covered without needing extra marinade.

Once marinated, peel the eggs to enjoy them as a snack or cut in half and add to soups or salads.

Tips

The eggs keep for about 4-5 days in the fridge so you can prepare a batch for the week or dole them out to friends. There are hundreds of variations on the recipe above and you can use different types of dark (hei cha) or black tea so feel free to experiment!

TEA SYRUP

Preparation time: 6 minutes, plus 30-60 minutes cooling // Cooking time: 5 minutes // Makes approximately 400ml

Tea syrups are a great and very easy way to incorporate a tea flavour into many food and drink items and can be stored for up to a month sealed in the fridge. We love to use these in any recipe where you would use a sugar syrup or flavoured syrup and they're also great with fluffy pancakes or added to cocktails, tonic or lemonades.

5g loose leaf Earl Grey tea

250ml boiled water

200g sugar

Steep the tea in the freshly boiled water for 6 minutes then strain into a saucepan. Place on the hob over a low heat. Add the sugar to the tea liquor and stir, heating gently, until it has dissolved. As a simple syrup for cocktails you're now done. Simply remove the pan from the heat, allow to cool and decant into your pouring bottle or storage jar.

If you're wanting a pouring syrup for desserts or to drizzle over pancakes, we think it's nice to thicken it a little, which is achieved by simply continuing to heat the syrup. This will concentrate the flavour and increase the viscosity. We like to reduce it by about a third for a slightly thicker syrup.

Note that as the syrup cools it will naturally thicken a little so don't go by the viscosity of the heated syrup and allow a little extra thickening from cooling. Once reduced sufficiently, allow to cool and decant into your pouring bottle or storage jar ready for use!

Tips

This recipe for Earl Grey syrup is amazing with fluffy pancakes and berry compote, but you can also switch to different teas for different effects. A rich, malty Assam syrup is great for pouring onto smoked bacon and chai syrup works with just about anything sweet!

TEA COMPOTES

Cooking time: 10-20 minutes // Preparation time: 5 minutes // Each recipe makes 400ml

Fruit compotes can bring a plain breakfast like yoghurt and granola or pancakes to life. They're SO easy to make and a great way to use up fruit that might be on its way out. In fact, slightly overripe fruit makes great compote and is quicker to break down. Add a flavourful tea to the mix for extra goodness; we've popped down three ideas below but go your own way with what you have in the house. These compotes will keep for about a week in a sealed jar in the fridge.

BLACK TEA AND MIXED BERRY COMPOTE

10g strong black loose leaf tea

100ml water at 100°c

500g frozen mixed berries

3 tbsp sugar

3 cloves

1 cinnamon quill

A lovely loose-textured rich compote that's great with yoghurt and also works well using a chai blend instead of the plain black tea. See the method on the next page.

STRAWBERRY, RASPBERRY & GREEN TEA COMPOTE

10g loose leaf green tea

100ml water at 80°c

500g ripe strawberries and raspberries

3 tbsp sugar

3 cloves

A lovely fresh summery treat that is almost a coulis, since the fresh berries will really break down. This also works really well with Earl Grey tea. See the method on the next page.

DRIED STONE FRUIT & GREEN TEA COMPOTE

Cooking time: 10-20 minutes // Preparation time: 5 minutes // Each recipe makes 400ml

Green tea works beautifully with dried fruit and adds depth of flavour to this chunky compote.

10g loose leaf green tea

600ml water at 80°c

500g mixed dried fruit like apricots, figs, sultanas and berries (halved or quartered if large)

1 tsp allspice

3 tbsp sugar

2 cloves

1 cinnamon quill

Toasted flaked almonds, for topping

Steep your tea in the hot water for 5 minutes and get everything else ready in the meantime. Add your fruit (if using frozen berries, add them straight from the freezer) to a pan over a medium heat, stir in the sugar (and any ground spices) then throw in the whole spices.

Pour the tea liquor into the pan and simmer until reduced. The liquid should be thick and syrupy. For fresh or frozen fruit this will take 5-10 minutes, for dried fruit closer to 20.

Once the compote is ready, remove from the heat and allow to cool. Remember to take out the whole spices before serving with yoghurt and granola or fluffy pancakes (see our recipe on page 74).

AROUND THE HOUSE

It's not just about eating and drinking tea. Here are some other ways to incorporate tea into your life: set some time aside, get creative and make something beautiful.

COSMETICS

Tea is not only a wonderful ingredient to eat and drink in its various forms, but thanks to its healing properties, antioxidants and fragrant nature, it's also brilliant in a range of cosmetics that you can make at home. We teamed up with Holmfirth's Our Tiny Bees to look at some easy DIY recipes including various teas, as well as our own Earl Grey soap.

SASSY NOIR BATH TEA

Preparation time: 10 minutes // Makes enough for about 4 baths

Did you know that bathing can diminish feelings of depression and pessimism? It creates a wonderful combination of isolation, quiet and comfort. If you're vegan, swap the milk powder for more bicarb or white clay powder.

50g goat's milk powder

100g sodium bicarbonate

20 drops of essential oil (lavender and rose work well)

10g cocoa butter, chilled

Handful of loose leaf tea

Place the milk powder and bicarbonate in a bowl, mix until well combined, then add the essential oil. Grate in the chilled cocoa butter (the finer the better) having refrigerated it for an hour or so to let it harden and become easier to grate. Add the tea of your choice and stir to combine.

Keep the bath tea in an airtight container (a 400ml jar should be perfect) and add a good handful to the water when you run a bath. Sit back, relax and enjoy the scent as well as a little moisturisation thanks to the cocoa butter.

JASMINE TEA FACE MASK

Preparation time: 10 minutes // Makes about 5 face masks

This is a perfect recipe to whip up when you want a little in-house spa treatment or pamper night! We've chosen simple ingredients that you can tweak any which way you like. Although this will keep in a fridge for a week, it may dry out, so it's best made fresh each time.

10g oats, powdered

10g loose leaf jasmine tea

50g white clay powder

6 drops of essential oil (frankincense, juniper, lavender and orange all work well with jasmine)

40ml water (or cooled jasmine tea)

Place the powdered oats and jasmine tea in a spice blender or similar and blend to a dust. Combine this with the clay powder in a small bowl and mix well. Add the essential oil and mix well. Stir in the water or tea 1 teaspoon at a time until the mixture is about the consistency of toothpaste.

Apply the face mask and leave on for around 15 minutes or until it has dried (you should see it pulling the oil out of your pores). Wash off and check out that glowing skin!

TEA CUPBOARD BODY SCRUB

Preparation time: 10 minutes // Makes approx. 250g

A lovely recipe that creates a pampering body scrub, perfect for moisturising and exfoliating in one. It can be used in the shower or bath, but be careful in the shower as it can make the floor a little slippery! Earl Grey adds a wonderfully fresh citrus zing that complements the scrub beautifully, leaving you thoroughly refreshed.

100g solid coconut oil

20ml macadamia oil (olive or sunflower can also work but are not as rich)

40 drops of essential oils (20 bergamot, 10 orange and 10 lemon works well)

120g unrefined dark brown sugar for a rougher scrub or Demerara for a gentler scrub

20g loose leaf Earl Grey tea

Mix the coconut oil and macadamia oil together (if the coconut oil is too hard for this, gently warm it slightly to soften it first). Give this mixture a good whip and it should become soft and fluffy. Add the essential oils and stir until combined, then stir in the sugar and tea until everything is well mixed.

This scrub will keep for 6 months in an airtight jar. In the shower or bath, simply take a handful and scrub away! Not only does this exfoliate but also leaves a lovely silky feeling on the skin. Pat yourself dry to keep some of the oils on your skin.

TEA BATH FIZZERS

Preparation time: 5 minutes // Makes 2 x 60mm bath bombs

This is a lovely project for all ages, so get the kids involved too! These fizzers make great gifts, are very simple to make and fill the air with an amazing scent when placed in the bath. All you need is a spray bottle and bath bomb moulds (widely available online) or simply use an ice cube tray.

150g sodium bicarbonate

75g citric acid

25g cornflour

5g loose leaf tea (Earl Grey, jasmine green tea or other sweet teas work well)

25 drops of essential oil (10 grapefruit, 10 bergamot and 5 lemon works well)

Combine the dry powders and tea in a bowl, pressing out any lumps so you have a well-mixed powder. Add the essential oils and mix again. Using a spray bottle filled with water, slightly dampen the mixture while stirring. It should start to form clumps, and is ready when it can be pressed together. Press the mixture into your bath bomb moulds or ice cube tray and then leave in a warm, dry place to harden before using. When your bath fizzers are ready, wrap them up to give away or pop one into a warm bath.

OUR TINY BEES

Our Tiny Bees make the most wonderful range of glorious, all-natural skincare that's good for you and good for British bees from their base just up the road from us, in Holmfirth. All products are 100% natural, cruelty-free, sustainable, and made in the UK and we've had a blast working with Jonathan to devise these wonderful recipes. Enjoy! Discover Our Tiny Bees at www.ourtinybees.co.uk or @ourtinybees on social media.

Earl Grey Soap

Tea Bath Fizzers

Tea Cupboard
Body Scrub

Jasmine Tea
Face Mask

Sassy Noir
Bath Tea

EARL GREY SOAP

Preparation time: 5 weeks // Makes 1 x 957g loaf

For detailed soap-making methods and recipes, we'd highly recommend Lovely Greens blog (lovelygreens. com/make-handmade-soap). Use this recipe as the quick guide and find out all about soaping temperatures, equipment and safety from Lovely Greens before commencing.

2.5g loose leaf Earl Grey tea

169.5g organic coconut oil

238.5g sustainable palm oil

271.5g olive (pomace) oil

192g cold water

96g sodium hydroxide (also known as lye or caustic soda)

15g organic bergamot oil

Equipment

Accurate weighing scales

1 large stainless steel pan or stockpot

1 medium-large Pyrex bowl

1 stainless steel food thermometer

1 stainless steel strainer

1 metal stick blender

Soap moulds (you can use household items like empty milk cartons if you don't want to buy moulds)

Health & Safety

Soap-making must be done in a well-ventilated space as caustic soda is very harmful if inhaled.

Use rubber gloves and wear goggles throughout your soap-making processes and for all further contact with the soap until it's completely ready, 5 weeks after production.

Read the precautions and follow all instructions on the lye/caustic soda packaging. Always put lye into water, **NEVER** water onto lye!

Blitz the tea leaves briefly in a food processor or pestle and mortar to get smaller pieces without turning them to dust. Carefully measure out all the ingredients into individual containers; do not use any more than the stated amount of bergamot oil. Open all windows and doors for ventilation.

Place the coconut, palm and olive oils in the large pan or stockpot and gently heat just enough to melt the solids. While they're warming through, put the cold water in the Pyrex bowl and then add the sodium hydroxide (NEVER the other way round). **CAUTION:** The mixture will fizz a lot and get hot as well as giving off lots of noxious gas so get out of the way for the initial burst!

Once the oils have melted, take them off the heat to cool down and keep a close eye on the temperatures of both the oils and the lye solution. You need them to be within 5-10°F of each other and close to 100°F (38°c). If the oils are cooling more quickly, you can pop them gently back on the heat for a few seconds but never heat the lye solution.

When both liquids are cool enough, strain the lye solution into the oils and mix with your stick blender until it starts to leave a trail behind. This will take anywhere from 5-15 minutes. It will test your arm strength (and patience)!

Now add the bergamot oil and mix for a further 30-60 seconds until the trace is more definite. Throw in your blitzed Earl Grey and stir well, then pour the liquid into the soap moulds. Wrap the moulds in a towel to insulate them, which helps the soap to cool evenly, and leave for 48 hours.

Once the soap has cooled and set, unwrap your bundle, de-mould the soap and, if you used a trough-style mould, slice into smaller bars using a cheese-wire, if you have one, or just a sharp knife. Place the bars slightly apart so that air can circulate around the surface. Leave for a minimum of 4-5 weeks, turning each bar over after 2 weeks, to ensure all the lye has saponified and none remains. This stage is crucially important.

Understand that you MUST leave your Earl Grey soap for a minimum of 4-5 weeks before using it. No shortcuts here.

When the soap is completely ready and safe to use, you can enjoy your creation! Test the soap on yourself first before wrapping the rest and giving them as wonderful gifts.

PRESSED WILDFLOWER & TEA LEAF ART

Preparation time: I hour, plus 4-6 weeks drying // Makes I frame

Create your very own framed artwork using ingredients you would find in tea. The tea leaves create a beautiful dark background to contrast bright colourful flowers against. In season, if you get any flowers on your Camellia Sinensis bush you can use these too. The creation photographed uses the 'ingredients' below but you can choose your own flowers or even recreate your own favourite tea blend in art form with fresh versions of the ingredients!

Fresh tea leaves on the stem

Buttercups

Mint

Bluebells

Hydrangea

Queen Anne's lace

Forget-me-nots

Daisies

Equipment

Wooden flower press or some heavy books

Blotting paper

Cardboard

Sharp scissors or secateurs

Tweezers

Contact adhesive or sticky dots

Frame of your choice with a hinge opening or a small amount of space between two panes of glass to suit the thickness of your flowers

Collect the plants and flowers for pressing, choosing a good variety of shapes and sizes. Prepare them by removing any dying or browning leaves and petals and removing stems of flowers that you are going to press 'face up'.

If you're using a flower press, unscrew the nuts from the bolts and remove the top panel of wood or, if using heavy books, start with one sturdy book at the bottom, then add a piece of card with blotting paper on top. Carefully lay some of your flowers and leaves flat on the blotting paper, taking care not to let any petals curl or bend under as this is how they will come out of the press when they are dry! Top with another layer of blotting paper and card and begin the next layer with a sheet of blotting paper again. Mix different types of flowers and leaves on each layer, keeping a few centimetres clear around the edge of each. Continue until you reach the capacity of your press or use up all your flowers. If you are using books, top the final layer with a couple of heavy books to weigh everything down.

Store your press or books in a warm, dry place with good airflow, checking on them regularly to make sure nothing is moulding. If you see any mould, remove the affected flowers and leaves as well as changing the paper to prevent further growth. Depending on the thickness of your flowers, they should be ready to be framed in around 6 weeks. Some may take longer, others less time, but this is a good general guide.

Carefully remove each layer of pressed flowers; they can be very delicate and tear easily so tweezers may be helpful when handling them. Open your display frame and carefully play around with layouts of the flowers you have pressed. Opt for a simple design with lots of space around each flower or layer them up for a fuller display.

Once you're happy with the look, secure each flower layer in place with a small dot of suitable glue, working as neatly as possible so the glue doesn't show. Alternatively, use self-adhesive sticky dots for less mess! Leave the glue to dry for the recommended time before closing your frame and admiring it!

KATIE SMART FLORAL ART

Smart Floral Art is a flower preservation studio located in Manchester that creatively presses, preserves and frames wedding bouquets in a modern and non-traditional way. Each piece is handmade to order and entirely unique, capturing your treasured memories to be admired for years to come. Katie is a true skilled artisan who makes the most incredible displays. Discover Smart Floral Art at www.smartfloralart.co.uk or @smartfloralart on social media.

TEA SCENTED CANDLE

Preparation time: 1 hour // Makes 1 candle

You don't have to drink or eat tea to enjoy it in your life. How about making your own tea scented candle? You can also add other essential oils or spices for additional aromas. This method works for any scent, so get out there and start experimenting!

50ml olive or coconut oil

10g loose leaf tea

Soy wax chips

Essential oils (optional)

Equipment

Saucepan

Metal sieve

Glass jar

Wooden or cotton candle wick

Slowly heat your oil in a small saucepan and then add the tea. Keep it hot for around 15 minutes until well infused and fragrant. Use the metal strainer or sieve to remove the tea from the hot oil, then fill your jar with soy wax chips and tip them into the oil. You can also drop in any essential oils here if you're using them. Stir the mixture as the wax chips melt until well combined.

If you're using a cotton wick, it's a bit easier to have the wick already in place before filling the jar. You can use a clothes peg to suspend it at the top so it stays in the centre.

Pour the scented wax mixture into your candle jar and, if needed, insert the wick until it reaches the bottom. Wait for the wax to set completely on a level surface and you're good to go!

ACKNOWLEDGEMENTS

We're incredibly proud of this book but we're certainly not the type to say "it was all us!"

We are indebted to many different people from all corners of the globe, from those who have helped us on our tea journey, hosted us at events, plied us with world class tea and invited us into their world with kindness and support (and tea!) to the masters of their craft who put unimaginable passion and devotion into growing the most beautiful teas for us to share with the world, to the retailers and cafés who proudly serve our teas and every single person who has ever bought tea from us at a market, café, shop or via our website.

To Stephen Carroll, who taught Owen's Tea Master Certification and took him under his wing, opening up a whole world of possibility, and to David Slater for giving our business a home.

Special thanks also to our beautiful and ever-patient wives, Summer and Mia, and to our children who fill us with love and inspiration each day. To our parents, to whom we owe it all and more, who constantly amaze us with their ongoing love and support, no matter how crazy we get. We love and admire more than you will ever know.

You have our hearts, forever. We hope we did you proud.

To all the people who helped directly in the making of this book.

Meze Publishing for holding our hand throughout this journey, for your excellent editing, photography and design support and for producing such a beautiful book.

To Peter and the team at PJ Taste and John at Parrot Club for bringing our recipes to life with your incredible cookery / mixology and for hosting our photoshoots.

And to every single person who contributed to our Crowdfunder campaign, no matter how little. It meant the world and without your support this book would never have happened.

Adam Harrison, Adam Riley, Adele Blair, Aiden Rigby, Alison Sheehan, Andrew Tucker, Anne and Richard Linton, Benjamin Colegrave, Benjamin Corbally, Beth Myers, Bhaveen Jobanputra, Caroline Burke, Catherine Keene, Chris Quy, Christine Freeman, Christine Robbin, Claire Narraway, Claire Pender, Clare Maxwell, David Hallas, David Stuart, Diana Brooks, Duncan Riley, Ellie LaCrosse, Emma Gladding, Erika Niko, Frances Parrish, Francesca Taylor, Gail Clarkson, Gail Hulett, Guy O'Brien, Hannah Calver, Hannah, Nik and Bump Patel, Harriet Coulthard, Hayley Walder, Hazel Mills, Hazel Riley, Helen Grimwood, Helen Johnson, Ian Brophy, James Hesketh, James Jenkinson, Janet Sharples, Jennifer Malone, Jennifer Rothwell, Jenny Johnson, Jeremy Pemberton, Jess and Conor, Joanna Roberts, Joanne Wharton, John Temple, Jules, Julian Rattigan, Julian Williamson, Katie Arundale, Katie Riley, Kirsty Smith, Lavinia Khan, Leila Sparrow, Lindsay Zoeller, Liz and Andy Houghton, Lloyd Eley-Smith, Louise Mckeon, Lucinda Weston, Maggie McQueen, Marc Appels, Martin Fairall, Mary Johnson, Matt Watts, Matthew Winslow, McBrockwin, Michael Rumsby, Mike Riley, Naomi Richardson, Nicola Hughes, Nicola Worthington, Olivia Allison, Paul Wills, Phoebe Harding-Walker, Richard Bayne, Richard Frodin, Robert Downham, Robin Southby, Rosemary Millican, Sacha Wright, Sadia Ur-Rehman, Sally J Crane, Sam Lloyd, Samantha Dunker, Sara Stansfield, Sean Johnson, Sewwie Tea, Siena Colegrave, Stefan Klueter, Steph Abiva, Stephen Brindley, Su Sutton, Sue Riley, Susan Morton, Tony Saunders, Victoria Evans, Victoria Smith, Will Noden.

From the bottom of our hearts, thank you.

Peace, love and tea.

Marc & Owen x